THE MEDICAL

How to
Break Into
Your
First Role

HUNDREDS OF
HIRING MANAGERS REVEAL
THE SECRETS FOR SUCCESS!

2nd EDITION

WORLD'S GREATEST JOB!

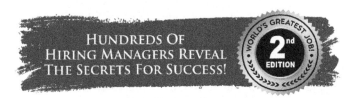

DR. SAMUEL JACOB DYER

Medical Science Liaison Inc.
Weston, Florida, USA

THE MEDICAL SCIENCE LIAISON CAREER GUIDE
How to Break Into Your First Role
Dr. Samuel Jacob Dyer

Second Edition
ISBN: 978-0-9899626-3-6 (trade paperback)
ISBN: 978-0-9899626-4-3 (ePub)
Also available for Kindle
Library of Congress Control Number: 2023943306

Editors: Sharon Honeycutt & Danielle Anderson
Indexing: Gina Guilinger, Weight of the Word Indexing Service
Cover design: Athur Sinai
Interior layout: Lighthouse24

Publisher's Cataloging-in-Publication Data
Names: Dyer, Samuel Jacob.
Title: The medical science liaison career guide : how to break into your first role : hundreds of hiring managers reveal the secrets for success! / Dr. Samuel Jacob Dyer.
Description: 2nd ed. | Weston, FL : Medical Science Liaison Inc., 2023.
Identifiers: LCCN 2023943306 | ISBN 9780989962636 (pbk.) | ISBN 9780989962643 (ePub)
Subjects: LCSH: Pharmaceutical industry—United States—Vocational guidance. | Biotechnology industries—United States—Vocational guidance. | Medical instruments and apparatus industry—United States—Vocational guidance. | Medical personnel—Vocational guidance. | BISAC: EDUCATION / Counseling / Career Development.
Classification: LCC HD9666.5 D94 2023 | DDC 615.1'023--dc23
LC record available at https://lccn.loc.gov/2023943306

Published by Medical Science Liaison Inc.
www.themslbook.com

Contents

Publisher's Note: This book refers to **Twitter** (now **X**) throughout, as the name change was announced after the pre-press production stage began. The Twitter links listed are valid as of the printing of this book and are expected to remain valid for the foreseeable future.

The difference between a successful person and others is not a lack of strength, not a lack of knowledge, but rather a lack of will.

Vince Lombardi

Preface

I have always been interested in the field of medicine. Although I was not interested in practicing medicine, I had always imagined having a career that was respected and directly involved in the latest medical advances. I also wanted a dynamic career that provided a high level of job satisfaction, global prospects, the opportunity to travel, significant autonomy, and financial rewards, as well as one that was in demand. When I began my career in the pharmaceutical industry in 2000, I found exactly what I was looking for in the Medical Science Liaison (MSL) role.

Prior to starting my career in the pharmaceutical industry, I was working in academia and had never heard of a Medical Science Liaison. Upon researching and learning about the profession, I decided it was exactly the career I had always wanted. Although I didn't have any contacts within the pharmaceutical industry or the MSL profession, I was determined to break into my first role utilizing drive and a lot of persistence. As I learned about the requirements for the position at various companies and the hiring preferences of individual MSL managers, I discovered specific techniques and developed effective strategies that enabled me to break into the MSL profession!

Throughout my pharmaceutical career, I used many of these same techniques and strategies to successfully progress from an MSL into MSL leadership, which included leading MSL teams and operations in over sixty countries and regions across the United States, Canada, Europe, Africa, the Middle East, New Zealand, and Australia. As a hiring manager, I also observed the techniques and strategies utilized by numerous successful aspiring MSLs from various academic and professional backgrounds.

In the first edition of this book, I shared all the techniques and strategies I developed during my career, as well as those I observed from successful aspiring MSLs. To date, the first edition of my book has helped launch the careers of hundreds of MSLs around the world and received hundreds of positive reviews from those who used the book to successfully break into their first MSL role.

Since the first edition was published, and while leading the Medical Science Liaison Society, I have gained unique insights into the hiring preferences of hundreds of MSL leaders from numerous companies, as well as additional insights into the specific techniques and strategies utilized by successful MSLs. As a result, I decided to update *The Medical Science Liaison Career Guide: How to Break into Your First Role* to share these additional insights and valuable information.

This new edition includes substantially more content regarding what it takes to break into the competitive MSL profession, including numerous new sections, several expanded sections, multiple updated templates, two new appendices, over sixty updated links, and ninety-five new tables revealing the results from several global surveys related to MSL hiring practices and other relevant information. Much of the data presented throughout this book has never been previously published.

My goal for writing the second edition of this book was the same as the first edition: to provide you with the tools, techniques, and strategies you need to compete and successfully break into this dynamic, rewarding profession.

Introduction

A Medical Science Liaison career provides substantial financial rewards, numerous benefits, professional growth, autonomy, and a high level of job satisfaction. As a result, MSL roles are highly sought after, and as you may have discovered, breaking into the MSL profession is very competitive! However, credible information on how to break in is scarce; thus, the MSL career remains elusive to many.

Even with the appropriate academic and professional background, breaking into the MSL profession can be a long, rigorous, and highly frustrating endeavor. It's nearly impossible to achieve on your own without the proper preparation and insights into the MSL hiring process.

So, how do you begin a career as an MSL? The Medical Science Liaison Career Guide: How to Break into Your First Role answers this elusive question! No other book provides a step-by-step guide on how to break into the MSL profession. Throughout this book, I will share strategies for distinguishing yourself from other applicants, including the secrets of how to successfully search for, apply for, interview for, and ultimately break into your first MSL role. I will also reveal the hiring preferences of MSL managers, as well as the most common reasons managers reject applicants throughout the hiring process.

Although MSLs are employed at multiple types of companies, including pharmaceutical, biotechnology, medical device, medical diagnostic, and other healthcare companies, the techniques I provide throughout this book can and should be utilized when researching, applying for, and interviewing for an MSL role at any company.

This book is divided into three parts designed to prepare you for each stage of the MSL hiring process.

Part 1—The Medical Science Liaison Role

In this section, you will learn the history and the purpose of the MSL role, how it has evolved, the typical activities of MSLs, and the future growth of the MSL profession. In addition, you will also discover details about breaking into the MSL profession from current MSLs. The information in this section will help you gain a clear understanding of the MSL profession and will help you set realistic expectations about what it will take to break into your first role.

Part 2—The MSL Job Search Strategy

In this section, you will learn the elements of a successful MSL job search strategy and what it takes to get noticed when applying for MSL roles. When applying for MSL positions, it's crucial to be strategic and methodical. As a result, I will share specific techniques for a successful job search strategy, including how to:
- Research the MSL role.
- Research the pharmaceutical industry.
- Research target companies.
- Research companies utilizing social media.
- Identify and develop an effective professional network.
- Leverage your professional network.

- Network virtually by strategically using LinkedIn, Twitter, and Facebook.
- Maximize attendance during in-person networking events or conferences.
- Write an effective MSL CV and cover letter that include the most relevant information.

The information in this section is critical for identifying and applying for MSL roles that match your professional background and scientific expertise, thereby increasing the chances you will be invited to interview.

Part 3—The MSL Hiring Process

In this section, you will learn the elements of a successful MSL interview strategy. Throughout the MSL hiring process, you must be thoroughly prepared. As a result, I will share specific techniques and strategies for each stage of the process, including:

- What to expect during each stage of the process.
- How to prepare for each interview.
- The most common questions asked during each type of interview.
- The questions you should ask a recruiter, someone from Human Resources (HR), the hiring manager, and other key decision-makers.
- How to prepare for and respond to behavioral questions.
- How to project professional body language during interviews.
- How to effectively prepare for the PowerPoint presentation during an in-person interview.
- The most common reasons MSL managers reject applicants during a phone interview and an in-person interview.
- How to write an effective thank-you letter after each interview.

I will also reveal what to expect during the offer stage, the components of a typical MSL offer letter, credible sources for MSL salary information, and effective salary negotiation tactics. The information in this section will be critical to your success throughout each stage of the MSL hiring process.

Appendices

In the book's appendices, you will learn the ten essential steps for a successful virtual interview; how large, medium, and small pharmaceutical companies are defined; and the differences between internal and external recruiters.

Although breaking into the MSL profession is very competitive, utilizing the numerous tools, techniques, and strategies I share throughout this book will significantly increase your chances of breaking into your first MSL role.

Part 1

The Medical Science Liaison Role

1   Past, Present, and Future of the MSL

As you begin to prepare for an MSL career, it's important to understand the history of the role, how it has continually evolved over the years, and the future impact that the role will have on the success of companies.

What is a Medical Science Liaison (MSL)?

A Medical Science Liaison (MSL) is a specific role within a pharmaceutical, biotechnology, medical device, medical diag-nostic, or other healthcare company. MSLs support a specific therapeutic area (e.g., oncology, neurology, rare/orphan diseases, endocrinology, immunology, etc.) and a specific disease state (e.g., lung cancer, Parkinson's disease, multiple sclerosis, diabetes, rheumatoid arthritis, etc.).

Medical Science Liaisons are vital to the success of companies and the products they support. They work throughout a product's life cycle, help to ensure products are utilized effectively, serve as scientific peers and resources within the medical community they support, and are scientific experts to internal colleagues at companies.

History and Purpose

The Medical Science Liaison (MSL) role was first established in 1967 by the Upjohn Company. The role was created in response to the need for a scientifically trained team capable of building collaborative relationships with influential physicians and other health care providers (HCPs), known in the pharmaceutical industry as key opinion leaders (KOLs).

Since its inception, the primary purpose of the MSL function has always been to foster ethical relationships with KOLs and other HCPs through the facilitation and exchange of valid, unbiased, truthful, and fair-balanced scientific information. MSLs accomplish this by providing an objective representation of all clinical data and scientific information regarding a particular disease, therapeutic area, or product.

Although originally called a Medical Science Liaison, over the years (and still today), companies have used various alternative titles for the role even though they have similar or equivalent responsibilities. You may encounter alternative titles when reviewing job descriptions or during an MSL interview. Some of these alternate titles include Field Medical Director, Regional Medical Liaison, Regional Medical Director, Medical Liaison, and Regional Scientific Manager, among others. However, "Medical Science Liaison" is still the most common title used for the role in the U.S. and globally (Table 1).

Companies also use various alternative titles for Key Opinion Leader (KOL) as well, including External Expert (EE), Thought Leader (TL), Medical Expert (ME), Key Thought Leader (KTL), and Opinion Leader (OL). You may also encounter these terms when reviewing job descriptions or during the various stages of the MSL interview process. However, a survey of 473 MSL professionals, which included executive management, MSL managers, MSL trainers, and MSLs from fifty-four countries revealed that "Key Opinion Leader," or KOL, is the most common term used globally (Table 2).

Table 1
Survey question: "There are numerous alternative titles for 'Medical Science Liaison.' What term does your organization use?"

U.S.	Alternative Professional Titles	Global
82%	Medical Science Liaison	79%
5%	Other (please specify)	6%
4%	Field Medical Director	3%
3%	Regional Medical Liaison	3%
2%	Regional Medical Director	2%
2%	Medical Liaison	2%
1%	Regional Scientific Manager	1%
0%	Regional Medical Advisor	1%
0%	Medical Advisor	2%
0%	Medical Science Manager	1%
0%	Medical Liaison Manager	1%

2018 "MSL Salary & Compensation Survey," MSL Society
1,655 MSL Professionals
U.S. and Global Results

Table 2
Survey question: "What term does your company use when referring to the physicians and other health care providers whose opinions are highly regarded and influence other physicians (sometimes referred to as KOL)?"

Alternative Titles for Influential Physicians			
Key Opinion Leader (KOL)	62%	Scientific Expert	2%
External Expert	8%	Therapeutic Area Expert	1%
Thought Leader (TL)	7%	I have no knowledge of this / Not applicable	0%
Medical Expert	6%	Disease Expert	0%
Other	4%	Expert Physician	0%
Key Thought Leader (KTL)	4%	Healthcare Expert	0%
Opinion Leader	4%	Scientific Consultant	0%
Health Care Provider (HCP)	2%	Scientific Collaborator	0%

2022 "The Best/Most Common Term Used for Key Opinion Leaders (KOL)," MSL Society
473 MSL Professionals
Global Results

Evolution of the Educational Background and Focus on Science

Historically, MSL teams consisted of individuals with various scientific backgrounds, including "super" pharmaceutical sales reps (i.e., those with scientific training who were highly successful), those with various educational levels (i.e., bachelor's or master's degrees in biology, nursing, etc.), and those with varying clinical experience. However, in the late 1980s, a number of pharmaceutical companies began to require those applying for MSL roles to have a doctorate degree, such as an MD, PharmD, or PhD. During this same period, a few governmental and nongovernmental agencies expressed concern regarding how pharmaceutical companies were engaging with physicians and HCPs. One of the concerns was specifically related to the perceived lack of differentiation between traditional sales and "educational" activities. These concerns had wide-reaching implications for the overall function and the specific activities of MSLs.

In the early 2000s, two significant guidelines addressing the interactions of pharmaceutical companies and health care professionals were published in the U.S. In 2002, the Pharmaceutical Research and Manufacturers of America (PhRMA), an organization based in the United States that represents research-based pharmaceutical and bio-technology companies, published its Code on Interactions with Health Care Professionals (https://www.phrma.org). These are commonly referred to as the PhRMA code guidelines. In 2003, the U.S. Department of Health and Human Services Office of Inspector General (OIG) published the Compliance Program Guidance for Pharma-ceutical Manufacturers (https://oig.hhs.gov). These are commonly referred to as the OIG guidelines.

Both guidelines were created—among other reasons—to ensure ethical practices and compliant behavior for interactions with health care providers. As a result, these guidelines address the concern that traditional commercial activities, such as sales and marketing, may influence the prescribing habits and other activities of physicians and HCPs. Ultimately, both of these initial guidelines, along with others that have been published since, have helped define the role and responsibilities of MSLs. Prior to these guidelines being published, many MSL teams were aligned with and functionally a part of the marketing or sales departments. However, after these guidelines were published, pharmaceutical companies began to create a distinct "firewall"—a separation between traditional commercial and medical educational activities. As a result, MSL teams at most companies were separated from commercial departments and realigned to become part of a distinct and independent medical affairs department to adhere to these new guidelines.

The Present

This organizational alignment has become the standard across pharmaceutical, biotechnology, medical device, and other companies that employ MSLs. The results of two surveys highlight the impact of these guidelines in the U.S. In 2004, 27 percent of companies surveyed revealed that their MSL teams were part of the sales and marketing departments, but in a 2010 follow-up study, that number had fallen to a mere 2 percent. Today, I am not aware of an MSL team that is part of the sales and marketing departments at any pharmaceutical company.

Doctorate Degrees: Now the Standard

Although a doctorate degree was not originally required for the MSL role, it has now become the educational standard for the profession globally. Prior to 2014, there is no historical data available to indicate the percentage of MSLs who had a doctorate degree, which would reveal when it became the educational standard. However, in 2014, the

Medical Science Liaison Society began conducting an annual global MSL Salary and Compensation Survey that included a question regarding the academic background of MSLs. Each year since its inception, the annual results have found that the vast majority of MSLs (across all years of experience) had a doctorate degree. The 2022 MSL Salary and Compensation Survey revealed that 89 percent of MSLs in the U.S. and 81 percent of MSLs globally had a doctorate degree (Tables 3 and 4).

Table 3
Survey question: "What is your highest academic background?"

Academic Background	
PharmD	42%
PhD	36%
MD/MBBS (or equivalent)	5%
Other Doctorate Degree (e.g., PsychD, DNP, etc.)	6%
Master's Degree (e.g., MS, MSN, etc.)	9%
Bachelor's Degree (e.g., BSN, BS, etc.)	2%
Other Degree (please specify)	2%

2022 "MSL Salary & Compensation Survey," MSL Society
1,032 MSLs/Sr. MSLs (or equivalent title)
U.S. Results

Table 4
Survey question: "What is your highest academic background?"

Academic Background	
PharmD	31%
PhD	39%
MD/MBBS (or equivalent)	7%
Other Doctorate Degree (e.g., PsychD, DNP, etc.)	4%
Master's Degree (e.g., MS, MSN, etc.)	15%
Bachelor's Degree (e.g., BSN, BS, etc.)	4%
Other Degree (please specify)	2%

2022 "MSL Salary & Compensation Survey," MSL Society
1,612 MSLs/Sr. MSLs (or equivalent title)
Global Results

The results of the 2022 MSL Salary and Compensation Survey also revealed that the percentage of new MSLs (those with less than one year of MSL experience) with a doctorate degree was even higher, which suggests it is increasingly more difficult to break into the MSL profession without a doctorate degree. In fact, the same survey found that 93 percent of new MSLs in the U.S. and 87 percent of new MSLs globally had a doctorate degree (Tables 5 and 6).

Table 5
Survey question: "What is your highest academic background?"

Academic Background	
PharmD	53%
PhD	25%
MD/MBBS (or equivalent)	5%
Other Doctorate Degree (e.g., PsychD, DNP, etc.)	10%
Master's Degree (e.g., MS, MSN, etc.)	4%
Bachelor's Degree (e.g., BSN, BS, etc.)	2%
Other Degree (please specify)	1%

2022 "MSL Salary & Compensation Survey," MSL Society
167 MSLs/Sr. MSLs (or equivalent title) with less than 1 year of experience
U.S. Results

Table 6
Survey question: "What is your highest academic background?"

Academic Background	
PharmD	41%
PhD	31%
MD/MBBS (or equivalent)	8%
Other Doctorate Degree (e.g., PsychD, DNP, etc.)	7%
Master's Degree (e.g., MS, MSN, etc.)	9%
Bachelor's Degree (e.g., BSN, BS, etc.)	4%
Other Degree (please specify)	<1%

2022 "MSL Salary & Compensation Survey," MSL Society
246 MSLs/Sr. MSLs (or equivalent title) with less than 1 year of experience
Global Results

One of the primary reasons a doctorate degree has become the educational standard for the profession is that MSL hiring managers think it should be required. In fact, a survey revealed that the majority of MSL hiring managers (in the U.S. and globally) reported a doctorate degree should be a requirement for the MSL role. Interestingly, although a doctorate degree is now standard, the majority of MSL hiring managers (in the U.S. and globally) also reported they do not have a preference for a specific doctorate degree when hiring (Tables 7 and 8).

Table 7
Survey question: "Which of the following academic qualifications do you prefer for MSLs? (Select One)"

Preferred Academic Qualifications	
PharmD	23%
PhD	18%
MD/MBBS (or equivalent)	13%
Other Doctorate Degree (i.e., PsychD, DNP, etc.)	1%
Nursing Degree	2%
No preference - I want a diversity of academic backgrounds on my team	42%

2018 "MSL Hiring Practices Survey," MSL Society
185 MSL Managers
Global Results

Table 8
Survey question: "Which of the following academic qualifications do you prefer for MSLs? (Select One)"

Preferred Academic Qualifications	
PharmD	32%
PhD	11%
MD/MBBS (or equivalent)	3%
Other Doctorate Degree (i.e., PsychD, DNP, etc.)	1%
Nursing Degree	2%
No preference - I want a diversity of academic backgrounds on my team	51%

2018 "MSL Hiring Practices Survey," MSL Society
97 MSL Managers
U.S. Results

Typical Responsibilities and Activities of MSLs

When the MSL role was created in 1967, the responsibilities of MSLs included various sales activities with high-prescribing physicians in support of approved drugs. However, today, MSLs no longer have any sales responsibilities, and they are commonly utilized to support both approved drugs as well as those in clinical development.

Typically, when a company launches an MSL team to support an approved drug or product, it will utilize the team for its most important drug or therapeutic area (be aware that at small companies, there may be only one drug or product). For example, pharmaceutical companies often utilize their MSL teams to support their "blockbuster drugs," which are commonly defined as drugs that have sales exceeding $1 billion USD annually. However, depending on the size and needs of the company, MSLs may also be utilized to support specialized products, such as "orphan drugs," which treat rare diseases or disorders. Alternatively, pharmaceutical companies may also utilize MSLs to support drugs in development, such as Phase II or Phase III compounds; these are molecules not yet approved by a regulatory body such as the Food and Drug Administration in the United States.

Regardless if a company utilizes its MSL team to support an approved drug or one in development, the activities of MSLs are typically primarily focused on fostering relationships with KOLs and HCPs through the exchange of unbiased, fair, and balanced scientific information. In fact, the results of a global survey revealed that the majority of MSL activities (both globally and in the U.S.) are directly or indirectly related to supporting or engaging with KOLs (Tables 9 and 10).

Table 9

Survey question: "Which of the following activities do you participate in? (select all that apply)"

Activity			
Attending medical conferences (and other conference support)	98%	Providing input for Medical Strategy	66%
KOL relationship management	98%	Tools development (slides, training materials, etc.)	65%
Educating KOLs and other Health Care Professionals	96%	Identify and training speakers	63%
Delivering scientific presentations	93%	Supporting and coordinating company sponsored research/trials	62%
Gathering Insights	90%	Material review (publications, educational materials, slides, etc.)	56%
Competitive intelligence gathering	76%	Continuing Medical Education (CME) activities	31%
Training and supporting sales force	76%	Medical publications	25%
Supporting investigator led research (IITs, ISTs, etc.)	74%	HEOR presentations or research	12%
Supporting Advisory Boards	73%	Managed Care activities	11%
Mentoring/training new MSLs	66%	Other (please specify)	2%

2022 "MSL Salary & Compensation Survey," MSL Society
1,612 MSLs/Sr. MSLs (or equivalent title)
Global Results

Table 10

Survey question: "Which of the following activities do you participate in? (Select all that apply)"

Activity			
Attending medical conferences (and other conference support)	99%	Supporting and coordinating company sponsored research/trials	66%
KOL relationship management	98%	Tools development (slides, training materials, etc.)	59%
Educating KOLs and other Health Care Professionals	98%	Providing input for Medical Strategy	59%
Gathering Insights	92%	Identify and training speakers	54%
Delivering scientific presentations	92%	Material review (publications, educational materials, slides, etc.)	51%
Competitive intelligence gathering	79%	Medical publications	20%
Supporting investigator led research (IITs, ISTs, etc.)	77%	Continuing Medical Education (CME) activities	18%
Mentoring/training new MSLs	72%	Managed Care activities	13%
Training and supporting sales force	71%	HEOR presentations or research	12%
Supporting Advisory Boards	69%	Other (please specify)	2%

2022 "MSL Salary & Compensation Survey," MSL Society
1,032 MSLs/Sr. MSLs (or equivalent title)
U.S. Results

As you research MSL roles, be aware that the specific activities and responsibilities of an MSL will vary across companies and will be determined by:

- The therapeutic area they support.
- Where a product is at in its lifecycle (i.e., in clinical development versus approved).
- Clinical strategy for the drug or product.
- The geographical location of the role.
- The company type (e.g., pharmaceutical, medical device, etc.).
- Other factors.

The responsibilities of an MSL team are generally categorized as (1) engaging external stakeholders, (2) collaborating with internal stakeholders, and (3) maintaining scientific knowledge. The specific activities associated within each category typically include the following:

1. Engaging External Stakeholders
   - KOL relationship management and engagement
   - Communicating medical or scientific data (e.g., delivering scientific presentations, educating KOLs and other health care providers, etc.)
   - Supporting advisory boards
   - Supporting investigator-led research (IITs, ISTs, etc.)
   - Identifying and training speakers
   - Supporting and coordinating company-sponsored clinical research
   - Supporting medical publications
   - Supporting managed care activities
   - Gathering insights
   - Health economics and outcomes research (HEOR) presentations
   - Continuing medical education (CME) activities

2. Collaborating with Internal Stakeholders
   - Training and supporting sales force on scientific or medical data
   - Mentoring and training new MSLs
   - Developing tools and resources (slides, training materials, etc.)
   - Reviewing materials (publications, educational materials, slides, etc.)
   - Providing input for medical strategies

3. Maintaining Scientific Knowledge
- Attending medical conferences (and other conference support)
- Gathering competitive intelligence
- Maintaining expertise in the therapeutic area and or disease state

A great resource to help you develop a clearer understanding of the various activities of MSLs is the Medical Science Liaison Guidelines published by the MSL Society. These guidelines are available for free on the MSL Society website. This document and how to access it will be covered in detail in Chapter 3.

The Future

Since being first established by Upjohn Pharmaceuticals in 1967, MSLs have become increasingly critical to the success of the companies that employ them. As a result, the MSL profession has grown exponentially over the last several years and is expected to continue to expand for the foreseeable future. In fact, a survey revealed that 68 percent of global MSL managers and 65 percent of U.S.-based MSL managers are planning to expand the size of their MSL team in the next two years (Tables 11 and 12).

Table 11
Survey question: "Are you planning to expand the size of the MSL team in the next 2 years?"

MSL Team Expansion Plans	
Yes	68%
No	32%

2018 "MSL Hiring Practices Survey," MSL Society
185 MSL Managers
Global Results

Table 12

Survey question: "Are you planning to expand the size of the MSL team in the next 2 years?"

MSL Team Expansion Plans	
Yes	65%
No	35%

2018 "MSL Hiring Practices Survey," MSL Society
97 MSL Managers
U.S. Results

Although it's clear the MSL profession will continue to expand, which will result in increased opportunities, you may be concerned if MSL managers are willing to hire someone without MSL experience. It's a valid concern. I guarantee (with rare exceptions) that every time you apply for an MSL position, you will be competing against experienced MSLs. However, a survey revealed that 86 percent of global MSL managers and 80 percent of U.S.-based managers have hired an aspiring MSL (Tables 13 and 14).

Table 13

Survey question: "Have you ever hired an aspiring MSL (someone without previous MSL experience)?"

MSL Hired with No Experience	
Yes	86%
No	11%
Not applicable; my company requires prior MSL experience	2%

2018 "MSL Hiring Practices Survey," MSL Society
185 MSL Managers
Global Results

Table 14
Survey question: "Have you ever hired an aspiring MSL (someone without previous MSL experience)?"

MSL Hired with No Experience	
Yes	80%
No	15%
Not applicable; my company requires prior MSL experience	4%

2018 "MSL Hiring Practices Survey," MSL Society
97 MSL Managers
U.S. Results

Importantly, this same survey also revealed that 84 percent of both global and U.S.-based MSL managers indicated they would also consider hiring an aspiring MSL in the future (Tables 15 and 16).

Table 15
Survey question: "Would you consider hiring an aspiring MSL (someone without previous MSL experience) in the near future?"

Consider Hiring Aspiring MSL	
Yes	84%
No	12%
Not applicable; my company requires prior MSL experience	3%

2018 "MSL Hiring Practices Survey," MSL Society
185 MSL Managers
Global Results

Table 16
Survey question: "Would you consider hiring an aspiring MSL (someone without previous MSL experience) in the near future?"

Consider Hiring Aspiring MSL	
Yes	84%
No	12%
Not applicable; my company requires prior MSL experience	4%

2018 "MSL Hiring Practices Survey," MSL Society
97 MSL Managers
U.S. Results

2

MSLs Reveal Details— Breaking into Their First Role

Understanding how current MSLs were successful in breaking into their first role, including information such as what sources they used, how long it took, and how many companies they applied to prior to breaking into the MSL profession, will help you create an effective job search strategy, as well as set realistic expectations. A global survey conducted by the MSL Society revealed insights into these important topics.

In 2018, 730 MSL professionals from fifty-six countries participated in the first MSL Hiring Practices Survey designed to better understand the current hiring practices for the MSL profession globally. I shared some of the results of this survey in Chapter 1. Throughout the remainder of the book, I will share additional results from this unique survey. The primary purpose of the survey was to gain useful insights into what the hiring process consists of from the perspectives of both MSL hiring managers and current MSLs across pharmaceutical, biotechnology, medical devices, and other healthcare companies.

The results of the MSL Hiring Practices Survey provide insights into what 185 MSL managers expect from applicants, as well as how they evaluate and analyze applicants. The results also reveal insights into what worked for 545 MSLs who successfully broke into the profession. All of these insights will be critically important to understand as you research, apply, and interview for MSL roles.

Understanding what sources MSLs utilize to find roles can help optimize your job search strategy. As you begin researching the MSL profession, you will discover there are multiple sources for MSL jobs, and it's likely you will need to utilize a combination of sources to find appropriate roles that match your background, including networking, social media, and job boards, among others. In fact, the Hiring Practices Survey revealed there is no single source utilized by the majority of MSLs either globally or in the U.S. (Tables 17 and 18).

Table 17
Survey question: "What source did you use to find your current MSL position? (Select One)"

Source Used to Find Current Job	
Recruiting/staffing firm	25%
Personal networking or referral (from a colleague/friend)	21%
Professional social media (LinkedIn)	16%
Referral from an employee of company	13%
Online job board/website (Indeed, CareerBuilder, Monster, etc.)	9%
Company website career page	6%
Other (please specify)	5%
Professional or medical organization website	2%
Networking event	1%
MSL Society job board	1%
Medical conference	1%
MSL/industry conference	<1%

2018 "MSL Hiring Practices Survey," MSL Society
545 MSLs (or equivalent title)
Global Results

Table 18
Survey question: "What source did you use to find your current MSL position? (Select One)"

Source Used to Find Current Job	
Recruiting/staffing firm	26%
Personal networking or referral (from a colleague/friend)	24%
Referral from an employee of company	14%
Professional social media (LinkedIn)	14%
Online job board/website (Indeed, CareerBuilder, Monster, etc.)	9%
Other (please specify)	5%
Company website career page	4%
Professional or medical organization website	1%
MSL Society job board	1%
Medical conference	1%
MSL/industry conference	1%
Networking event	<1%

2018 "MSL Hiring Practices Survey," MSL Society
303 MSLs (or equivalent title)
U.S. Results

The total amount of time required to search, apply, and interview for MSL roles will vary depending on numerous factors, including the:

- Availability of roles in your therapeutic area or disease state expertise.
- Total number of MSLs being hired for a company's team.
- Number of applicants being considered for each role.
- Schedule and availability of multiple decision makers.
- Urgency of the company needing to fill roles.
- Other factors.

As a result, the overall process of searching, applying, and interviewing for MSL roles can be lengthy. In fact, the majority of experienced MSLs (those with years of experience), both globally and in the U.S., revealed it took up to four months to break into their first role, whereas the majority of new MSLs (those with less than one year of MSL experience), both globally and in the U.S., revealed it took up to six months to break into their first role (Tables 19–22). These results suggest that breaking into the profession is increasingly more difficult and competitive, and they underscore the importance of having an effective job search strategy (which is covered in detail later in the book).

Table 19
Survey question: "Before breaking into your first MSL role, how long had you applied/searched for MSL roles?"

MSL Job Search Time	
Less than 1 month	24%
1 month	6%
2 months	5%
3 months	10%
4 months	4%
5 months	2%
6 months	14%
7 months	1%
8 months	1%
9 months	1%
10 months	2%
11 months	0%
12 months	5%
1 - 1.5 years	8%
1.5 years - 2 years	5%
2+ years	6%
I don't recall	5%

2018 "MSL Hiring Practices Survey," MSL Society
545 MSLs (or equivalent title)
Global Results

Table 20
Survey question: "Before breaking into your first MSL role, how long had you applied/searched for MSL roles?"

MSL Job Search Time	
Less than 1 month	24%
1 month	7%
2 months	5%
3 months	11%
4 months	5%
5 months	2%
6 months	15%
7 months	<1%
8 months	2%
9 months	1%
10 months	1%
11 months	0%
12 months	5%
1 - 1.5 years	8%
1.5 years - 2 years	4%
2+ years	7%
I don't recall	5%

2018 "MSL Hiring Practices Survey," MSL Society
303 MSLs (or equivalent title)
U.S. Results

Table 21

Survey question: "Before breaking into your first MSL role, how long had you applied/searched for MSL roles?"

(MSLs with less than 1 year of MSL experience)

MSL Job Search Time	
Less than 1 month	8%
1 month	8%
2 months	6%
3 months	7%
4 months	6%
5 months	1%
6 months	15%
7 months	0%
8 months	1%
9 months	1%
10 months	5%
11 months	0%
12 months	8%
1 - 1.5 years	15%
1.5 years - 2 years	6%
2+ years	11%
I don't recall	2%

2018 "MSL Hiring Practices Survey," MSL Society
87 MSLs (less than 1 year of MSL experience)
Global Results

Table 22
Survey question: "Before breaking into your first MSL role, how long had you applied/searched for MSL roles?"
(MSLs with less than 1 year of MSL experience)

MSL Job Search Time	
Less than 1 month	10%
1 month	10%
2 months	6%
3 months	8%
4 months	8%
5 months	2%
6 months	13%
7 months	0%
8 months	2%
9 months	2%
10 months	6%
11 months	0%
12 months	4%
1 - 1.5 years	15%
1.5 years - 2 years	4%
2+ years	10%
I don't recall	2%

2018 "MSL Hiring Practices Survey," MSL Society
52 MSLs (less than 1 year of MSL experience)
U.S. Results

It's likely you will interview for multiple MSL roles before successfully breaking into the profession. In fact, the majority (55 percent globally and 53 percent in the U.S.) of MSLs reported they interviewed with two or more companies before breaking into their first role. Interestingly, more than 20 percent of MSLs, both globally and in the U.S., interviewed with four or more companies before breaking into their first role (Tables 23 and 24).

Table 23
Survey question: "How many companies did you interview with (phone or in-person) before you broke into your first MSL role (including the company that hired you)?"

Number of Companies Interviewed With	
1 Company	45%
2 Companies	19%
3 Companies	16%
4 Companies	8%
5 Companies	6%
6 Companies	2%
7 Companies	1%
8 Companies	1%
9 Companies	<1%
10 Companies	1%
10+ (please specify)	1%

2018 "MSL Hiring Practices Survey," MSL Society
545 MSLs (or equivalent title)
Global Results

Table 24
Survey question: "How many companies did you interview with (phone or in-person) before you broke into your first MSL role (including the company that hired you)?"

Number of Companies Interviewed With	
1 Company	47%
2 Companies	17%
3 Companies	17%
4 Companies	7%
5 Companies	5%
6 Companies	2%
7 Companies	1%
8 Companies	2%
9 Companies	<1%
10 Companies	2%
10+ (please specify)	1%

2018 "MSL Hiring Practices Survey," MSL Society
303 MSLs (or equivalent title)
U.S. Results

Finally, it's important to have a realistic expectation of the length of the MSL hiring process (which includes the time from first applying to a company until receiving an offer letter). As with the overall process of searching, applying for, and interviewing for MSL roles, the time required for the MSL hiring process will likely be lengthy. In fact, 51 percent of MSLs globally and 48 percent of MSLs in the U.S. reported the hiring process took two months or longer to complete (Tables 25 and 26). For some roles, it may take much longer. Interestingly, 31 percent of MSLs globally and 24 percent of MSLs in the U.S. reported the hiring process took three months or longer to complete.

Table 25

Survey question: "Regarding your first MSL role, how long did it take from when you first applied to the company until you received the offer letter? (i.e., how long was the application/hiring process)"

Hiring Process Length	
Less than 1 month	25%
1 month	22%
2 months	19%
3 months	16%
4 months	5%
5 months	2%
6 months	3%
7 months	1%
8 months	<1%
9 months	<1%
10 months	<1%
11 months	0%
12 months	<1%
13 months	0%
14 months	0%
15 months	<1%
16 months	<1%
17 months	0%
18 months	1%
I don't recall	4%

2018 "MSL Hiring Practices Survey," MSL Society
545 MSLs (or equivalent title)
Global Results

Table 26
Survey question: "Regarding your first MSL role, how long did it take from when you first applied to the company until you received the offer letter? (i.e., how long was the application/hiring process)"

Hiring Process Length	
Less than 1 month	27%
1 month	24%
2 months	23%
3 months	15%
4 months	4%
5 months	2%
6 months	1%
7 months	1%
8 months	0%
9 months	0%
10 months	0%
11 months	0%
12 months	<1%
13 months	0%
14 months	0%
15 months	<1%
16 months	0%
17 months	0%
18 months	<1%
I don't recall	2%

2018 "MSL Hiring Practices Survey," MSL Society
303 MSLs (or equivalent title)
U.S. Results

Part 2
The MSL Job Search Strategy

3 The Importance of Research

Before you begin applying for MSL roles, it's crucial to thoroughly research and have a clear understanding of the role, the industry, and the specific companies to which you will apply. Your best chance of breaking into your first MSL role will be by matching your scientific expertise to the specific companies that specialize in your therapeutic area or disease state.

In this chapter, you'll learn the four critical steps to researching appropriate MSL roles, the industry, and target companies. These steps are crucial because during the interview process, the hiring manager and others from the company (Human Resources, marketing, sales) will expect you to have knowledge about the company's therapeutic areas, their products—including the indications and uses—and other specific information unique to the company.

Even if the hiring manager or others do not directly ask about your knowledge of the company and its products, they will nevertheless be assessing this based on your answers to questions throughout each interview. Your inability to demonstrate company or product knowledge may be perceived as a lack of interest in, or knowledge of, the company. As a result, discussing information about the company and its products is an effective way to distinguish yourself from other applicants who are not as well prepared.

One of the keys to a successful interview, and ultimately breaking into the MSL profession, is preparation. In fact, 87 percent of MSLs globally and 89 percent of U.S.-based MSLs revealed they "strongly agreed" or "agreed" that researching and demonstrating knowledge of the company and/or company product(s) during the interview process was very important to breaking into the MSL role (Tables 27 and 28).

Table 27
Survey question: "Researching and demonstrating knowledge of the company and/or company product(s) during the interview process was very important in breaking into the MSL role."

Importance of Company Knowledge	
Strongly Agree	53%
Agree	34%
Neutral	10%
Disagree	2%
Strongly Disagree	1%

2018 "MSL Hiring Practices Survey," MSL Society
545 MSLs (or equivalent title)
Global Results

Table 28
Survey question: "Researching and demonstrating knowledge of the company and/or company product(s) during the interview process was very important in breaking into the MSL role."

Importance of Company Knowledge	
Strongly Agree	55%
Agree	34%
Neutral	9%
Disagree	2%
Strongly Disagree	<1%

2018 "MSL Hiring Practices Survey," MSL Society
303 MSLs (or equivalent title)
U.S. Results

Not only is preparation a critical contributing factor to successfully breaking into the MSL profession, but insufficient preparation will also jeopardize your chances of moving forward in the interview process. Many hiring managers disqualify applicants who cannot or do not demonstrate knowledge of the company and its specific product(s). In fact, according to a survey conducted by the MSL Society, almost half (49 percent) of U.S.-based MSL managers reported that a "Lack of knowledge of the company and/or our product(s)" is one of the most common reasons that prevent them from moving an applicant forward in the hiring process.

Over the years, I have interviewed numerous candidates who lacked specific knowledge about the drug or therapeutic area and, as a result, were unable to discuss these critical details. In every occasion that this occurred, it was simply due to a lack of research and preparation. For example, during an interview, one candidate asked me what the drug was indicated for! This individual had clearly not prepared for the interview, and it was a complete waste of my time, along with the time of my colleagues who had already interviewed him. It was also a complete waste of the money the company had spent to get him to the interview (including flight, hotel, taxis, and food expenses). Overall, it was simply unprofessional. Due to his lack of preparation, I immediately dismissed him as a potential hire. For the remainder of the interview, it did not matter what he said; my mind was already made up—he was clearly not a good fit for my team.

Lack of preparation will not only, almost certainly, result in you being eliminated from consideration, but it will also make each interview more stressful. Don't make this critical mistake! Use the techniques in the following section to fully prepare for each interview.

Essential Steps to Successful Research

Step 1. Research the MSL role. Read job descriptions, MSL research, and published articles about the MSL role.

Step 2. Research the pharmaceutical industry. Familiarize yourself with major industry trends and news, regulations, disease state updates, the indications for which drugs are approved, and the financial health (most importantly the profitability) of the pharmaceutical industry.

Step 3. Research target companies. Identify companies whose products or drug pipeline focus on your therapeutic area or disease state expertise.

Step 4. Research companies using social media. Keep updated on target companies and industry news, and follow key decision makers.

Although it's not necessary to utilize all the following resources listed for each step, they may help in your preparation and research. Let's look at each step in more detail.

Step 1: Research the MSL Role

As you may have already discovered, credible, accurate, and reliable information specific to the MSL role is scarce and can be difficult to find.

During your research, it's imperative that you understand both the most common activities of an MSL, as well as how companies utilize the role to fit their own business and strategic needs.

You will need this information because during each interview the hiring manager and others (e.g., Human Resources, recruiter, etc.) will:

✓ Expect you to be able to discuss the role and its function at the company.

✓ Expect you to understand and possibly discuss how the MSL role differs from other field-based roles, such as sales reps.

- ✓ Expect you to demonstrate your understanding of how the role engages with KOLs and other HCPs.
- ✓ Discuss the MSL's role in the clinical development of the specific drug or therapeutic area.

Medical Science Liaison Society

The Medical Science Liaison Society (MSL Society) has members in more than one hundred countries and is the only 501c3 nonprofit organization dedicated to advancing the global MSL profession. The MSL Society offers numerous resources exclusively for the MSL profession that will help you gain a better understanding of the role, including:

- ✓ Hundreds of presentations from MSL leaders.
- ✓ 200+ global reports on various topics related to the MSL profession (e.g., typical MSL activities, how MSLs are engaging with KOLs, how MSLs are being utilized, metrics used to evaluate MSL performance, MSL job satisfaction, compliance, etc.)
- ✓ An annual global MSL Salary and Compensation Report.
- ✓ Webinar recordings with MSL leaders discussing issues impacting the MSL profession.
- ✓ Other resources.

All of these resources are accessible through professional-level membership. Reviewing them is a great way to gain a better understanding of the MSL role (www.themsls.org).

Medical Science Liaison Activity Guidelines

In 2018, the MSL Society published the first-ever official guidelines for Medical Science Liaison Activities. The information provided in this document is designed to provide guidelines for appropriate internal and external activities of Medical Science Liaisons, and it contains information generally applicable to the global profession. These guidelines clearly describe and define the MSL role and the typical activities and responsibilities of MSLs, and they established standards to ensure that MSL activities are primarily focused on:

- Fostering ethical relationships with KOLs.
- Facilitating the exchange of valid, unbiased, fair, and balanced scientific information within the context of a medical product or device and the therapeutic area the MSL supports.

As mentioned previously, reviewing the Medical Science Liaison activity guidelines will help you develop a greater understanding of the MSL role. This document is available for free on the MSL Society website at www.themsls.org/msl-guidelines. As you research, apply, and interview for MSL roles, I strongly recommend that you review these guidelines to gain a thorough understanding of the MSL function.

The MSL Journal

The MSL Journal is the official publication of the Medical Science Liaison Society and is the only journal or publication exclusively focused on the MSL profession. The journal is available complimentary to the public at **themsljournal.com**. *The MSL Journal* features original articles and content focusing on:

- ✓ Professional development.
- ✓ Insights from MSLs and MSL leaders.
- ✓ Global survey results and analysis.
- ✓ Industry news and trends.
- ✓ MSL best practices.
- ✓ MSL job postings.

Reading *The MSL Journal* is an easy way to stay updated and gain insights into issues impacting the MSL profession. Being able to discuss relevant topics from recent published articles in *The MSL Journal* is a great way to demonstrate your understanding of the MSL role and to distinguish yourself from other applicants during interviews.

Sources for MSL Job Descriptions

While the activities of MSLs will vary across companies, reading and comparing MSL job descriptions is an effective way to understand the differences between various roles. MSL job descriptions can be found on numerous websites, including the following sources:

- MSL Society job board (http://careercenter.themsls.org)
- Indeed (www.indeed.com)
- Glassdoor (glassdoor.com)
- CareerBuilder (Careerbuilder.com)
- Monster (monster.com)
- PharmiWeb (www.pharmiweb.com)
- Seek (www.seek.com.au)
- LinkedIn (www.linkedin.com)
- Individual pharmaceutical company websites

Annual MSL Society Conference

The Annual MSL Society Conference is the largest gathering of MSL professionals (https://themsls.org/annual-conference). This event is a valuable resource for understanding what is being discussed globally about the MSL role and is a unique opportunity to network with MSLs and MSL leaders. Although this meeting is designed and intended for MSLs and MSL management, as an aspiring MSL, attending the conference will provide a unique opportunity to learn from, meet, and network with numerous MSLs and MSL managers. As I will share later, networking is critical to successfully breaking into your first role.

Step 2: Research the Pharmaceutical Industry

The pharmaceutical industry is one of the most financially successful global industries in history, with many companies having multiple multibillion dollar products. However, it's also one of the most highly regulated industries in the world and requires multiple functions (including medical affairs, sales, marketing, regulatory affairs, and research and development) to work together to make a company successful. Researching the pharmaceutical industry is essential because during the interview process, a hiring manager will likely expect you to be able to:

✓ Discuss what drugs are being investigated and/or what drugs have been approved in the therapeutic area or disease state the MSL role supports.

✓ Discuss what drugs are being investigated and/or what drugs have been approved in the therapeutic area or disease state at competitor companies.

✓ Understand and generally discuss the drug approval process, the governmental agencies and regulations involved, and the medical and business implications.

✓ Understand and discuss trends in the industry.

✓ Identify which companies are the global leaders for the disease state the MSL role supports.

✓ Discuss how a company's drug(s) compares with its competitors from both a medical and a business standpoint.

✓ Understand and discuss the product lifecycle and how drug patents affect this from medical, sales, and marketing perspectives.

There are several resources you can utilize to obtain this information. What follows are some of the best and most highly regarded resources available.

Top Pharmaceutical Publications and Blogs

There are numerous blogs and publications focused on the pharmaceutical industry. The following are some of the most popular resources that publish the latest industry news and trends.

- **American Pharmaceutical Review:** http://www.americanpharmaceuticalreview.com/
- **Applied Clinical Trials:** www.appliedclinicaltrialsonline.com
- **Biospace:** www.biospace.com
- **Bloomberg Health-Care Blog:** https://news.bloomberglaw.com/health-law-and-business
- **Check Orphan:** https://checkorphan.org
- **The European Federation of Pharmaceutical Industries and Associations (EFPIA):** https://efpia.eu
- **FDA Law Blog:** www.thefdalawblog.com
- **Fierce Biotech:** www.fiercebiotech.com
- **Fierce Pharma:** www.fiercepharma.com
- **Journal of Medical Marketing:** http://mmj.sagepub.com
- **Nature Biotechnology:** https://www.nature.com/nbt
- **Pharma Times:** http://www.pharmatimes.com/
- **Pharma Voice:** www.pharmavoice.com
- **Pharmaceutical Executive:** www.pharmexec.com
- **Pharmaphorum:** www.pharmaphorum.com
- **PM360:** www.pm360online.com
- **Wall Street Journal Health Blog:** www.wsj.com/news/life-work/health-wellness

Regulations and Guidelines

Several global agencies dictate how pharmaceutical companies market their products and how their employees interact with physicians and other health care providers. It's not practical to list them all, but the following are the regulatory agencies for the largest global pharmaceutical markets.

- **The U.S. Food and Drug Administration:** www.fda.gov
- **The Pharmaceutical Manufacturers Association:** www.phrma.org
- **U.S. Department of Health and Human Services, Office of Inspector General (OIG):** https://oig.hhs.gov/
- **The Office of Prescription Drug Promotion (OPDP):** https://www.fda.gov/about-fda/center-drug-evaluation-and-research-cder/office-prescription-drug-promotion-opdp
- **The European Medicines Agency (EMA)** (similar to FDA, but for the European Union): www.ema.europa.eu
- **Therapeutic Goods Administration (TGA)** (similar to FDA, but for Australia): www.tga.gov.au
- **Japanese Ministry of Health, Labour and Welfare** (similar to FDA, but for Japan): https://www.mhlw.go.jp/english/

Clinical Trial Information

The following resources provide information on the drugs and indications that are being investigated in a particular disease state in both publicly and privately supported clinical studies.

- **ClinicalTrials.gov:** http://www.clinicaltrials.gov/
- **National Institutes of Health:** www.nih.gov
- **Center Watch:** www.centerwatch.com/

Drugs for Specific Medical Conditions

The following sources provide up-to-date information on the approved indications and usage for medications.

- **Monthly Prescribing Reference:** https://www.empr.com/
- **Drugs.com:** www.drugs.com/medical_conditions.html
- **Medscape:** https://reference.medscape.com/

- Pharmaceutical company websites that have approved drugs for a specific condition
- **U.S. Drug Development and Approval Process:** https://www.fda.gov/Drugs/DevelopmentApprovalProcess/default.htm

Latest Disease State Updates

The following are great resources to access the latest clinical research from a broad range of therapeutic areas and disease states.

- **The Journal of the American Medical Association:** https://jamanetwork.com/
- **New England Journal of Medicine (NEJM):** www.nejm.org
- **Nature Medicine:** www.nature.com/nm/
- **British Medical Journal:** www.bmj.com/
- **The Lancet:** www.thelancet.com
- **Annals of Internal Medicine:** annals.org/aim
- **Mayo Clinic:** www.mayoclinic.com
- **The Merck Manual:** www.merckmanuals.com/professional
- Any specific pharmaceutical company website
- Medical society websites for specific conditions
- Medical journals focused on specific diseases or conditions

General Business

It's necessary to have a general understanding of the financial health (most importantly the profitability) of a company, especially if you are interested in a small company that may have only one approved product. Pay particular attention to their best-selling products (if they have multiple products), their competitors, what makes their product(s) unique, and what drugs they have in development.

- **Google Finance:** www.google.com/finance
- **Yahoo! Finance:** finance.yahoo.com

- *The Wall Street Journal*: www.wsj.com
- **CNN Money**: www.money.cnn.com
- *Forbes*: www.forbes.com

Best Company Lists

The following are some resources that will help you begin to understand how individual pharmaceutical companies are perceived by their employees and which companies are regarded as the best places to work. However, you should be aware that the best company to work for is the one that will hire you!

- *Science*: https://www.sciencemag.org/features/2020/10/top-employers-rapid-response-covid-19-diversity-and-innovation
- *Fortune*: www.greatplacetowork.com/best-workplaces/100-best/2020
- *Inc. Magazine*: https://www.inc.com/inc5000
- *Forbes*: www.forbes.com/lists/best-regarded-companies/

Step 3: Research Target Companies

As you begin to research and identify target companies, you will discover they are frequently described as large, medium, small pharma, or biotech, with varying definitions (see Appendix A for further details). The size of a therapeutic area can vary widely as well. Some therapeutic areas have multiple drugs that treat millions of patients, whereas other therapeutic areas, such as orphan diseases, may have a single drug that treats only hundreds of patients with a rare condition.

Regardless of how a company is described or the size of their therapeutic area, when you are identifying a target company, the most important criteria is ensuring the company's products or drug pipeline focus on your therapeutic area or disease state expertise. For example, if your education or work experience has been in the area of oncology or HIV, you will need to research and identify the companies that focus on your therapeutic area or disease specialty. This is important because, as I mentioned, your best chance of breaking into your first MSL role will be by matching your scientific expertise to the specific companies that specialize in your therapeutic area or disease state.

This research will also be helpful throughout the interview process because during each interview the hiring manager will expect you to:

✓ Discuss the disease state(s) the company is focused on as well as specific products within the therapeutic area.

✓ Demonstrate that you are up to date on the drugs in development (pipeline), as well as any relevant company news.

✓ Discuss how your professional expertise in a disease state or therapeutic area matches the requirements for the role.

After you have identified target companies, you need to thoroughly study the company by utilizing the resources previously mentioned and the company website, concentrating on the following sections and information:

✓ Company facts and figures

✓ Annual report

✓ Drugs or products in development (pipeline)

✓ Key approved and marketed drugs or products

✓ Career section

✓ Management page

✓ Company announcements

Company Facts and Figures

✓ What is the company's history, mission, and goal(s)?

✓ What is the company's primary therapeutic area or disease state focus?

✓ How does the company differentiate itself from its primary competitors?

✓ Is it a global or national company?

✓ Where are the global headquarters located?

Annual Report:

If the company's annual report is not on its website, it can be obtained by contacting the company directly. You should familiarize yourself with the following facts:

✓ Total sales

✓ Total revenue

✓ Sales volume

✓ Market share in your therapeutic area

✓ Profit

✓ Total number of employees

Drugs or Products in Development (Pipeline)

✓ How many drugs or products does the company have in its pipeline in your area of expertise?

✓ At what various clinical phases are the drugs in development?

Key Approved and Marketed Products

✓ What are the company's best-selling products?

✓ Does the company have any blockbuster products?

✓ How many marketed products does the company have?

✓ How long have these brands been on the market?

✓ How many marketed products does the company have in your area of expertise?

✓ What are the approved indications for the product(s) in your area of expertise?

Career Section

- ✓ How many MSL job openings are currently listed in your area of expertise?
- ✓ How does the MSL job description for your area of expertise compare with those at other companies?
- ✓ If the company has MSL openings in different therapeutic areas, how do they compare? Are the roles and responsibilities similar?
- ✓ Do you understand and are you able to discuss in detail the key elements of the MSL role in your area of expertise? (Remember that each company utilizes its MSL team a little differently.)

Management Page

- ✓ Review the bios of the executive management.
- ✓ Review the organizational structure.
- ✓ Read the bios of the medical affairs executive leadership.

Company Announcements

- ✓ Latest news
- ✓ Press releases
- ✓ New product launches
- ✓ Executive management changes and announcements
- ✓ Latest regulatory agency approvals (e.g., FDA in the U.S.)

Researching a Company's Approved and Marketed Drug(s) or Product(s)

After reviewing the previous information, you should look at the specific therapeutic area, medical condition, and the drug(s) that match your background. Generally, there are two sections for products on a company website: (1) patient information pages and (2) prescriber or doctor information pages. Review both sections to gain an understanding of how the product is marketed as well as the science of the drug. Patient information pages often have several resources, including marketing materials, patient information brochures, videos, and other general information. The prescriber information pages focus on the science of the drug, details regarding the various clinical trials conducted to obtain approval (if applicable), and other specific prescribing information.

In this section, you will also generally find what is known in the U.S. (and in other countries as well) as the "Prescribing Information," or simply PI. In the U.S., this is a legal document approved by the Food and Drug Administration (FDA) that dictates every marketing and sales message about a drug that a company is allowed to state or advertise.

The following is the key information you need to know and should be able to discuss with a hiring manager and others about a product:

- ✓ What is the drug's regulatory agency (e.g., FDA in the U.S.) approved indication(s)?
- ✓ When was it approved for its indication(s)?
- ✓ Do you understand, and could you explain, the science (pharmacology) behind the drug?
- ✓ What is the drug classification?
- ✓ Do you understand, and could you explain, why this drug is important and unique medically or scientifically?
- ✓ What are the medical and scientific advantages of a company's drug?
- ✓ What are the primary competitors to the drug?
- ✓ What are the medical and scientific advantages of the competitors' drugs?

✓ What makes this company's product different from its competitors from both a medical and scientific and a marketing perspective?

An easy tool for researching target companies and keeping updated on key information is utilizing Google alerts. You can set up a Google alert for any term, including a target company, their products, the disease state, etc. After setting up an alert, you will receive an email anytime that term appears in new Google search results.

Step 4: Research Companies Utilizing Social Media

Social media tools are useful for staying up to date on the latest company news and developments. Most pharmaceutical, medical device, and biotechnology companies have a presence on popular social media sites. Utilize these sites to get the latest company updates, to follow key decision makers and executive leaders, and to connect to target companies. Using social media can help you prepare to discuss the latest company news and developments throughout the interview process.

In the next chapter, I will expand on the importance of all of this, including the most effective ways to utilize the most popular social media sites when researching and applying for MSL roles.

The Power of Focused Networking

4

"**I**t's not what you know, but who you know that matters." This quote is almost a cliché. Some may mistakenly interpret this statement to mean that experience and expertise are not important. However, this quote emphasizes the importance of having a network of professionals who are familiar with your specific skills, accomplishments, qualifications, and potential fit for a particular role. Having a focused network will be invaluable in breaking into the MSL role.

As you have already discovered from previous chapters, you will not successfully break into your first MSL role simply by searching job boards or applying for roles on company websites. Breaking into the MSL career will require you to utilize a variety of techniques involving both passive and active strategies, including effective networking.

What Is Networking?

Networking is the process of establishing contacts and building relationships with those who have related professional interests. Networking is commonly cited as an important aspect of a successful job search strategy across all professions and is one of the most essential components of a successful MSL job search strategy. In fact, a survey revealed that 76 percent of MSLs globally and 78 percent of U.S.-based MSLs "agree" or "strongly agree" that networking was important to their success in breaking into the MSL role (Tables 29 and 30).

Table 29
Survey question: "Networking was important to my success in breaking into the MSL role."

Importance of Networking	
Strongly Agree	51%
Agree	25%
Neutral	14%
Disagree	8%
Strongly Disagree	2%

2018 "MSL Hiring Practices Survey," MSL Society
545 MSLs (or equivalent title)
Global Results

Table 30
Survey question: "Networking was important to my success in breaking into the MSL role."

Importance of Networking	
Strongly Agree	56%
Agree	22%
Neutral	12%
Disagree	8%
Strongly Disagree	3%

2018 "MSL Hiring Practices Survey," MSL Society
303 MSLs (or equivalent title)
U.S. Results

How to Identify and Develop an Effective Professional Network

The strategy commonly advised when searching for a new career opportunity is to network with everyone, including family, friends, acquaintances, and colleagues. However, as you begin to develop a professional network for the purpose of breaking into the MSL profession, the most effective networking strategy will result from focusing on those directly involved with the MSL community. While you do not want to exclude any potential contact, your focus should include recruiters, Human Resources, MSLs, MSL managers, or anyone else directly involved with the MSL community. Your personal network within the MSL community will likely be as important to your job search strategy as your academic background, therapeutic area, or disease state experience.

Leveraging Your Network

Knowing how to approach people within your network and how to leverage them is equally as important as building your network. Unfortunately, many aspiring MSLs do not recognize the importance of networking, nor do they know how to develop and leverage their network. Ultimately, the primary goal of focused networking is to leverage your contacts to increase your chances of breaking into the MSL career. Throughout the process of researching and applying for MSL roles, you should leverage your network for multiple purposes, including:

- Gaining knowledge about the pharmaceutical, biotechnology, or medical device industry.
- Introductions and connections with other MSL professionals in their networks.
- Being a source of information about the MSL profession.

- Offering MSL career advice.
- Mentoring.
- Helping you identify appropriate, open MSL roles at a company.
- Serving as an internal referral for an MSL role at a company.
- Providing information about a specific company and insights into its culture.

When communicating with your network, you should be clear about what you are trying to achieve and be specific with any requests. However, avoid the temptation of focusing only on your needs by asking about job opportunities. This approach can put those you are reaching out to in the awkward position of having no information to offer or not being able to help. Remember that networking is about creating connections and building relationships. Successful networking consists of information exchange and should always be reciprocal in nature. As a result, although you should utilize your network for information, potential job opportunities, or career advice, you should also always be willing to support those in your network by sharing information or connecting people when appropriate.

Virtual Networking and Utilizing Social Media to Build an Online Presence

Networking online is an integral part of an effective MSL job search strategy. Although in-person networking will remain important, using social media to network online will be the primary way you develop and communicate with your network.

Social media is one of the most common sources MSL hiring managers and recruiters utilize to search for candidates. In fact, although MSL managers utilize a variety of sources to obtain applicants, 69 percent of MSL managers globally and 68 percent of U.S.-based MSL managers indicated that they (or their organizations) use LinkedIn, making it a primary source for identifying candidates for MSL positions (Tables 31 and 32). As a result, having a professional online presence will be imperative to your success.

Table 31
Survey question: "What sources do you or your organization utilize to obtain applicants for MSL positions? (Select all that apply)"

Applicant Recruitment Sources	
Employee referrals	77%
Recruiting/staffing firms	76%
Referrals from within your personal network	72%
LinkedIn	69%
Company website career page	67%
Online job boards (Indeed, CareerBuilder, Monster, etc.)	27%
Networking events	25%
MSL/industry conferences	17%
Professional or medical organization websites	9%
MSL Society job board	6%
Facebook	3%
Internal recruiter	2%
HR Deparment	1%

2018 "MSL Hiring Practices Survey," MSL Society
185 MSL Managers
Global Results

Table 32
Survey question: "What sources do you or your organization utilize to obtain applicants for MSL positions? (Select all that apply)"

Applicant Recruitment Sources	
Employee referrals	86%
Referrals from within your personal network	78%
Recruiting/staffing firms	74%
Company website career page	70%
LinkedIn	68%
Online job boards (Indeed, CareerBuilder, Monster, etc.)	26%
Networking events	22%
MSL/industry conferences	21%
MSL Society job board	11%
Professional or medical organization websites	9%
Internal recruiter	4%
Facebook	3%
HR Deparment	2%

2018 "MSL Hiring Practices Survey," MSL Society
97 MSL Managers
U.S. Results

Having a social media presence enables both hiring managers and recruiters to further research your background and to learn more about you and your potential fit with a role. These sites also enable you to further highlight your relevant skills and experiences. The majority of MSL managers utilize social media to evaluate MSL applicants. In fact, 61 percent of MSL managers globally and 63 percent of U.S.-based MSL managers "always" or "often" use social media to research/evaluate applicants for MSL roles (Tables 33 and 34).

Table 33
Survey question: "How often do you use Social Media (LinkedIn, Facebook, etc.) to research/evaluate applicants for the MSL roles you are hiring for?"

Social Media Use in Evaluation	
Always	32%
Often	29%
Sometimes	21%
Rarely	10%
Never	8%

2018 "MSL Hiring Practices Survey," MSL Society
185 MSL Managers
Global Results

Table 34
Survey question: "How often do you use Social Media (LinkedIn, Facebook, etc.) to research/evaluate applicants for the MSL roles you are hiring for?"

Social Media Use in Evaluation	
Always	37%
Often	26%
Sometimes	24%
Rarely	9%
Never	4%

2018 "MSL Hiring Practices Survey," MSL Society
97 MSL Managers
U.S. Results

Although there are numerous social media sites, LinkedIn, Facebook, and Twitter are the three most important sites used by MSL managers, recruiters, and those in HR to research and evaluate MSL applicants. These three sites have revolutionized the way pharmaceutical, biotechnology, medical device, and other healthcare companies recruit MSLs, as well as how applicants interact with companies. Knowing how to effectively use these sites will be crucial to successfully developing an MSL-focused network. What follows are some of the most effective techniques for utilizing these social media sites.

Strategies for Using LinkedIn, Twitter, and Facebook

LinkedIn

LinkedIn is the largest professional social media site in the world with hundreds of millions of members. It is the most commonly used social media site within the business community and has become the preferred site for professionals to build an online professional network. As a result, LinkedIn is the simplest, most effective, and easiest way to build an online professional presence and to develop an MSL-focused network.

With a LinkedIn profile, you can easily develop a network by connecting directly with hiring managers, recruiters, and others within the MSL community. Your profile enables those in your network, as well as others who search your name, to learn more about you. LinkedIn is also an effective tool for researching hiring managers and other key decision makers within a company prior to an interview.

Hiring managers, recruiters, those working in HR, and other decision makers are active on LinkedIn, and you should be as well. It's highly likely that when you apply for an MSL role, those reviewing your application will also utilize the site to further evaluate your background and experience as a potential fit for the role. As an MSL manager, I personally searched LinkedIn for every single MSL candidate I ever interviewed. Utilizing LinkedIn to review and evaluate MSL applicants has become a standard practice among MSL managers. In fact, 80 percent of MSL managers globally and 83 percent of U.S.-based MSL managers reported that they use LinkedIn when evaluating MSL applicants (Tables 35 and 36).

Table 35
Survey question: "Select the platforms that you utilize to review when evaluating MSL applicants (Select all that apply)."

Platforms Utilized	
LinkedIn	80%
None of these	15%
Facebook	15%
Google+	12%
Other (please specify)	10%
Twitter	7%
Blogs	6%
MSL Society global directory	5%

2018 "MSL Hiring Practices Survey," MSL Society
185 MSL Managers
Global Results

Table 36
Survey question: "Select the platforms that you utilize to review when evaluating MSL applicants (Select all that apply)."

Platforms Utilized	
LinkedIn	83%
Facebook	17%
Google+	15%
Other (please specify)	12%
Twitter	11%
None of these	10%
Blogs	9%
MSL Society global directory	8%

2018 "MSL Hiring Practices Survey," MSL Society
97 MSL Managers
U.S. Results

Although there are multiple articles on LinkedIn (and other sources) regarding how to effectively utilize the platform, the following are fifteen essential steps for maximizing your LinkedIn presence:

1. Register if you don't already have an account. The site offers both a free basic membership and an upgraded premium subscription, which offers many advantages, including the ability to see who has viewed your profile, as well as the opportunity to contact those who are outside your immediate network. You should review the information from the LinkedIn Learning Center, including the FAQ, which provides additional information on getting started on the site.

2. Customize your public profile URL. You can change the last part of the automatically generated public URL for your profile to your name. For example, I changed mine from www.linkedin.com/pub/your-name/31/73b/a91 to www.linkedin.com/in/samueldyer. A customized URL appears much more professional when someone reviews your profile or when you are sharing your LinkedIn URL with others. You should add your personal LinkedIn URL to the top of your CV and to your email signature to make it easier for those interested to learn more about you (I will share further details in Chapter 5).

3. Complete your profile. LinkedIn enables you to build a profile that highlights your professional experiences, specific accomplishments, skills, education, and other relevant details. Ensure your profile is complete and updated, including a well-written "About" section, your education details, a complete work history, and a listing of your skills. In addition, include publications (in which you are a listed author) that highlight your experience in a specific therapeutic area and/or disease state.

4. Use a professional photo. According to LinkedIn, adding a profile photo makes your profile fourteen times more likely to be viewed by others when conducting LinkedIn searches.

The following are several recommendations to consider when selecting an appropriate professional photo:

- Use a current photo.
- Utilize a professionally taken photo; do not use a selfie.
- Use a high-resolution image (400x400 pixels).
- Look approachable; smile with a natural expression.
- Use a headshot in which your head and face occupies 60 percent of the photo.
- Avoid group photos; be the only person in the picture.
- Avoid distracting backgrounds.
- Wear professional business attire (refer to the "What to Wear" section in Chapter 7).
- Don't incorporate hobbies, pets, or any props in your photo.

5. Add a background image. Your profile photo and background image will be the first details someone sees when they view your profile. Having an appropriate image that highlights your relevant MSL skills may help you stand out from others, grab the reader's attention, and be more memorable. For example, an image of you presenting data would be a great way to demonstrate your communication and presentation skills.

6. Use an appropriate headline. The headline section at the top of your profile allows customization of your title which may improve the visibility of your profile within the MSL community. Your photo and headline are the most visible details of your profile because they are included in all search results on the platform. Although the headline section is customizable, ensure it is not misleading. Some aspiring MSLs mistakenly list their title in the headline section as "MSL" or "Medical Science Liaison." However, 87 percent of global and

94 percent of U.S.-based executive leaders and MSL managers revealed in a survey that it's unprofessional and misleading when an aspiring MSL uses "Medical Science Liaison" as their professional title on their LinkedIn profile before actually breaking into the profession (Tables 37 and 38).

Table 37
Survey question: "Do you think it's unprofessional and misleading when an aspiring MSL uses 'Medical Science Liaison' as their professional title on their LinkedIn profile before actually breaking into the role (i.e., refer to themselves as an MSL before breaking in)?"

Unprofessional/Misleading Use of "Medical Science Liaison" title	
Yes	87%
No	13%

2021 MSL Society Survey
123 Executive Management/Vice President of Medical Affairs and Manager/Director of MSLs (or equivalent title)
Global Results

Table 38
Survey question: "Do you think it's unprofessional and misleading when an aspiring MSL uses 'Medical Science Liaison' as their professional title on their LinkedIn profile before actually breaking into the role (i.e., refer to themselves as an MSL before breaking in)?"

Unprofessional/Misleading Use of "Medical Science Liaison" title	
Yes	94%
No	6%

2021 MSL Society Survey
79 Executive Management/Vice President of Medical Affairs and Manager/Director of MSLs (or equivalent title)
U.S. Results

Table 39
Survey question: "Is 'Aspiring Medical Science Liaison' an appropriate professional title to use on one's LinkedIn profile for someone trying to break into the role?"

Appropriateness of "Aspiring Medical Science Liaison" title	
Yes	72%
No	28%

2021 MSL Society Survey
125 Executive Management/Vice President of Medical Affairs and Manager/Director of MSLs (or equivalent title)
Global Results

Table 40
Survey question: "Is 'Aspiring Medical Science Liaison' an appropriate professional title to use on one's LinkedIn profile for someone trying to break into the role?"

Appropriateness of "Aspiring Medical Science Liaison" title	
Yes	70%
No	30%

2021 MSL Society Survey
81 Executive Management/Vice President of Medical Affairs and Manager/Director of MSLs (or equivalent title)
U.S. Results

7. Write a powerful "About" section. Appropriately utilizing this section is an effective way to strengthen your profile and differentiate yourself from other aspiring MSLs. Some elements of a powerful "About" section include:

- Using this section to tell your story.
- Starting strong with an attention-grabbing statement.
- Highlighting your unique skills and experience relevant to the MSL profession.
- Utilizing keywords and relevant search terms (e.g., therapeutic area, disease state, etc.).
- Listing achievements that will have the biggest impact and are the most relevant to the MSL profession (e.g.,

presentations given at a scientific conference focusing on the same therapeutic area or disease state).

- Using short paragraphs.
- Using bullet points for key information.
- Keeping it professional and avoiding the use of special characters.

8. Embed keywords throughout your profile. Keywords are often used by MSL managers, recruiters, and those in HR to search for qualified candidates. As a result, it's crucial to incorporate keywords throughout your profile that are relevant to the MSL profession. These keywords should be the same as the search terms or phrases that hiring managers or other key decision makers would use when searching for candidates, including the specific therapeutic area, disease state, name of a drug, etc. Incorporating relevant terms increases the chances that your profile will be viewed when managers or others search the site for individuals with backgrounds similar to yours. To become familiar with the potential keywords that may be searched, review MSL job descriptions in your therapeutic area or disease state. Another tactic is to search and review LinkedIn MSL profiles within your therapeutic area to familiarize yourself with common keywords used.

9. Utilize recommendations. These can be an effective way to further highlight and validate your competencies, skills, and expertise in your therapeutic area and/or disease state. Ask for recommendations from current and former managers or colleagues that highlight your skills and knowledge that are most relevant to the MSL profession (e.g., teamwork, presentation and communications skills, therapeutic area and/or disease state expertise, etc.). You should also be willing to write recommendations when appropriate because

it can demonstrate your ability to build meaningful, long-term relationships.

10. Make your profile public. You can control how much information in your profile is displayed on LinkedIn by adjusting the profile settings to public or private. Ensure all sections of your profile are publicly visible so that your profile will appear in search results on LinkedIn, as well as search engines like Google, Bing, etc.

11. Build an MSL-focused network. Although LinkedIn allows you to connect with anyone on the site, the most effective networking strategy will result from connecting with those directly involved with the MSL community. A simple technique to find appropriate connections within the MSL community is to type "Medical Science Liaison" into the search bar on the site. The search results will include MSLs, MSL managers, recruiters, and others who have used "Medical Science Liaison" as keywords in their headlines, titles, or profiles. You can then sort and filter the results by several different categories, including their location, current or past companies, and industry, among others. After identifying someone with whom you would like to network, you can either "follow" their profile or "connect" with them from the search results page. When building your connections on LinkedIn, it's essential to focus on the quality of your first connections rather than the overall number of connections.

Additional simple techniques to build your network on LinkedIn include:

- Invite everyone you speak to within the profession (e.g., MSLs, recruiters, and others) to connect with you on the site.

- Anytime someone refers a name to you as a potential contact within the profession, immediately search for that person on LinkedIn, and send them an invitation to connect, if appropriate.

12. Search MSL jobs. You can search for MSL jobs from target companies by clicking on the "Jobs" icon on the top menu when logged into LinkedIn. Type "Medical Science Liaison" into the search function. Narrow the results by searching by location, company, date posted, and other filters. Target companies can also be found by typing the most relevant keywords for your specific therapeutic area in the advanced search bar. For example, if your specialty is oncology, you can type terms such as "Medical Science Liaison oncology" or "MSL oncology" into the search bar to identify companies hiring in that area.

    Before applying for any MSL role, determine if you are connected on LinkedIn to the individual who posted the position or to anyone else (e.g., an MSL, the hiring manager, etc.) who works at that company. For some job postings, LinkedIn will display who posted the job and your degree of connection with that individual. If you are directly connected to the individual who posted the job, contacting that individual prior to applying may provide further insights into the position. Alternatively, if you are not directly connected, utilize your network of individuals who work at the company to obtain further information about the role prior to applying. Leveraging your LinkedIn network using these techniques may ultimately strengthen your application.

13. Connect with the hiring manager. Prior to attempting to connect with the hiring manager for a role for which you have applied or for which you are actively interviewing, it is

important to determine when it is appropriate to connect. The appropriate timing for sending a connection request depends on the individual hiring manager and the stage of the application and interview process.

Interestingly, according to a survey, 33 percent of global MSL managers and 30 percent of U.S.-based MSL managers reported it is appropriate to connect "anytime" during the interview process. However, the majority of MSL managers (51 percent globally and 61 percent in the U.S.) revealed it is only appropriate "after an in-person interview" or "after receiving an offer letter" (Tables 41 and 42).

Table 41
Survey question: "At what point during the interview process is it appropriate for an applicant to connect with you (as the hiring manager) on professional social media (e.g., LinkedIn, MSL Society)? (Select all that apply)"

When to Contact Manager	
After learning who the hiring manager is for the role	6%
After a phone interview has been scheduled, but has not yet occurred	4%
After a phone interview	6%
After an in-person interview	22%
After receiving an offer letter	29%
Anytime	33%
Never	8%

2018 "MSL Hiring Practices Survey," MSL Society
185 MSL Managers
Global Results

Table 42
Survey question: "At what point during the interview process is it appropriate for an applicant to connect with you (as the hiring manager) on professional social media (e.g., LinkedIn, MSL Society)? (Select all that apply)"

When to Contact Manager	
After learning who the hiring manager is for the role	5%
After a phone interview has been scheduled, but has not yet occurred	3%
After a phone interview	4%
After an in-person interview	21%
After receiving an offer letter	40%
Anytime	30%
Never	4%

2018 "MSL Hiring Practices Survey," MSL Society
97 MSL Managers
U.S. Results

When appropriate, sending a brief message to the hiring manager expressing your interest in the role can make a positive impression when several potential candidates are being considered. If you decide to send a message, consider the following guidelines:

- Use appropriate titles, such as Dr., Mr., Mrs., or Ms.
- Don't misspell the recipient's name.
- Don't use emojis.
- Keep it concise; limit your message to a maximum of four to five sentences.
- Keep your message formal and professional in style and tone.
- Express enthusiasm for the specific position, and mention if you have already applied.
- Highlight how your skills and experience match the requirements of the role listed in the job description.
- Before sending the message, proofread it for spelling, typos, and grammatical errors.

14. Join relevant MSL-focused groups. LinkedIn allows you to join a maximum of one hundred groups. You can search for MSL-focused groups by name or keyword, or you can browse groups that LinkedIn recommends. Be aware that LinkedIn groups are categorized as "listed" (public) or "unlisted" (private) which is determined by individual owners and/or managers. Only the listed groups will appear in the search results. Only members of each group can view group content, including discussion posts, polls, videos, and job posts.

    There are many groups dedicated to the pharmaceutical industry, medical devices, medical affairs, and even specific disease states or therapeutic areas. There are also a number of LinkedIn groups you can join that are dedicated to MSLs, including the Medical Science Liaison and Medical Affairs Networkers (www.linkedin.com/groups/1813731/). This is the largest group on LinkedIn focused on medical affairs and MSLs, which is a great resource for networking. Joining relevant groups will enable you to connect with people within the MSL community who are working at target companies. Being a member of relevant groups enables you to gain insights into industry trends and the MSL profession, while simultaneously helping you build your network.

    Be aware that requests to join a group may require approval from the group owner or manager(s). As a result, your request to join a particular group may not be approved. However, if you are not approved, simply send a message to the group owner and request approval, explaining that you are pursuing the MSL career, and you would like to join the group.

    As you join each group, search fellow members and request a direct connection with anyone who might be a valuable contact. In addition, after joining a group, become active by liking relevant posts and participating in discussions when appropriate.

15. Be active. Being active on LinkedIn provides multiple benefits, including the ability to connect directly with MSL professionals, and enabling you to both learn more about the MSL profession and/or discover MSL job opportunities. In addition, being active by sharing relevant content and/or adding appropriate comments to posts can help raise your visibility within the MSL community.

However, avoid commenting on or posting casual and/or personal content on the following topics:
- Politics
- Entertainment
- Sports
- Dating
- Family news
- Religion
- Other personal or nonbusiness topics

Instead, when posting content, publishing articles, or commenting on others' posts, share information that demonstrates your enthusiasm for the MSL profession, a specific disease state, a therapeutic area, or a target company. When determining what is relevant and appropriate to post, consider the following types of content:
- Therapeutic area or disease state updates (e.g., a recent article that has been published)
- Target company news
- Quotes from MSL leaders or executives from target companies
- Images (e.g., disease pathway, etc.)

- Infographics (e.g., demographics, incidence, the prevalence of a disease, etc.)
- Videos (e.g., disease process, mechanism of action, etc.)
- Upcoming medical conferences or other relevant events
- MSL skills development (e.g., any relevant training you have completed, including certificates, etc.)

Twitter

This social media networking platform has hundreds of millions of registered users. Twitter utilizes instant messaging, which allows you to connect with individuals or companies and communicate quickly using short text messages (under 280 characters) called "tweets." Most pharmaceutical companies and many recruiters utilize Twitter and will often tweet about job openings. As a result, Twitter is increasingly being utilized as a part of an effective job search strategy that includes the ability to:

- Build an online professional presence.
- Discover MSL job opportunities.
- Research target companies.
- Build an MSL-focused network.
- Read industry news.
- Gain career advice.
- Share information with your network.

The following are ten essential steps for maximizing your Twitter presence:

1. Register using your personal email address. However, don't use an unprofessional personal email address, such as awesomemsl@gmail.com. Avoid using a work-related email address.

2. Customize your Twitter handle by using your full first and last name, if possible. This creates a more professional appearance and will help other users more easily find you on Twitter. If someone has already registered with your name, try incorporating an underscore in your handle.

3. Add a link to an external professional profile, such as your LinkedIn account or to a personal website like yourname.com. This will enable those reviewing your profile to learn more about you. For more information on a personal website, see "Additional Method for Building an Online Presence" later in this chapter.

4. Write a professional bio. Write a bio that highlights your most relevant experience and accomplishments related to the MSL profession utilizing relevant keywords. For consistency, you can use part of your LinkedIn profile summary for your Twitter profile.

5. Use a professional photo. For consistency, use the same photo for all your professional online profiles. Refer to the "LinkedIn" section in this chapter for specific recommendations to consider when selecting an appropriate professional photo.

6. Search for MSL jobs. An easy method for searching for MSL jobs on Twitter is to simply type "medical science liaison jobs" in the Twitter search bar.

7. Communicate only professional messages. When communicating on Twitter through direct tweets, retweeting, or replying to tweets, always maintain a professional image. Avoid communicating anything that may be considered controversial, polarizing, or offensive. Refer to the "LinkedIn" section in this chapter for specific recommendations regarding topics to avoid.

8. Share your expertise. When you tweet, share information about industry-related topics or your area of expertise. This will enable you to further establish your online presence and add value to those in your network. Refer to the "LinkedIn" section in this chapter for specific recommendations regarding relevant and appropriate types of content.

9. Follow target companies and individuals. There are several advantages to following target companies and individuals (e.g., recruiters, MSL managers, executives, HR professionals, etc.), including potentially discovering new MSL job postings, the ability to communicate directly with those who you follow, and keeping updated on the latest company or industry news (which may help you prepare for interviews). When you follow an individual or a company, they will receive a notification that they have a new follower, which may prompt them to view your profile.

10. Turn on mobile alerts. After following a target company or individual, be sure to turn on mobile notifications. This will ensure that you receive an alert on your phone whenever a company or individual you are following posts a tweet— including new job postings.

Facebook

Facebook is the largest social media site in the world, with billions of users. The platform allows you to create an account, connect with others, and share information. Although originally intended for personal use, Facebook is increasingly being utilized by companies and recruiters to post company updates, news, and MSL job opportunities. As a result, you can easily develop an MSL-focused network on Facebook by connecting directly with hiring managers, recruiters, and others within the MSL community.

If you decide to use Facebook for professional networking or to search for jobs, you will need to consider your privacy settings because every action on the site has sharing and privacy implications. Due to Facebook's "Community Standards," prohibiting an individual from maintaining two separate personal accounts (e.g., for the purposes of personal and professional networking), the following are three options for utilizing your Facebook account:

1. *Use Facebook exclusively for personal connections*
   With this option, it's crucial to ensure your privacy settings are set, so no one has access to your profile except those in your private network. However, be aware that even when you restrict who can see what you share on the site, hiring managers, recruiters, those working in HR, or others may search for your profile, so verify how your public profile appears and what content is visible, including comments on posts, images shared, and posts.

2. *Use Facebook exclusively for professional networking*
   With this option, you will eliminate all private social interactions with friends, family, and other personal contacts. This will require removing all personal information from your profile, including family status, age, personal photos, etc. that you may not want hiring managers, recruiters, someone from HR, or others to see. After editing your profile information, begin building an MSL-focused network on the site.

3. *Use Facebook for both personal connections and professional networking*
   With this option, you will need to carefully consider what photos, comments, and other content you share to ensure you're projecting a professional image. You will need to either continually monitor all content posted on your timeline, as well as all content in which you are tagged, or adjust your

privacy settings so that all posts in which you are tagged and all content posted on your timeline requires your approval. Refer to the "LinkedIn" section in this chapter for specific recommendations regarding relevant and appropriate types of content.

Additional Method for Building an Online Presence

In addition to utilizing social media, those reviewing your application may also conduct an internet search for your name to learn more about you. As an MSL manager, I conducted a Google search on every person I interviewed for an MSL role. In fact, 88 percent of global MSL managers and 87 percent of U.S.-based MSL managers "always," "often," or "sometimes" conduct an online search utilizing Google, Bing, etc. to research and/or evaluate applicants (Tables 43 and 44).

Table 43
Survey question: "How often do you conduct an online search utilizing Google, Bing, etc. as part of the research/evaluation of applicants for the MSL roles you are hiring for?"

Frequency of Online Searching	
Always	24%
Often	25%
Sometimes	39%
Never	12%

2022 MSL Society Survey
163 Manager/Director of MSLs (or equivalent title)
Global Results

Table 44
Survey question: "How often do you conduct an online search utilizing Google, Bing, etc. as part of the research/evaluation of applicants for the MSL roles you are hiring for?"

Frequency of Online Searching	
Always	22%
Often	26%
Sometimes	39%
Never	13%

2022 MSL Society Survey
85 Manager/Director of MSLs (or equivalent title)
U.S. Results (Data collected from 2022-03-31 and 2022-05-06 webinars)

As a result, it's imperative to have an online presence in addition to your social media profiles. Purchasing the .com domain for your first and last name and creating a personal website can be an effective technique to make it easier for those conducting internet searches for your name to learn more about you. If the .com for your first and last name is not available, use a creative yet professional variation, such as drfirstlastname.com or firstlastnamephd.com. Your personal website should include highlights of your professional experiences, accomplishments, skills, education, and other details that are relevant to the MSL role. There are several platforms for creating simple personal websites, such as wordpress.com. You can then add your personal website to your LinkedIn account under the contact information section at the top of your LinkedIn profile.

In-Person Networking

As with virtual networking, the most effective in-person networking strategy will result from connecting with those directly involved with the MSL community (e.g., MSL, MSL manager, recruiter, etc.). Therefore, when considering attending an in-person conference or event, focus on those that will likely include attendees or speakers from the MSL profession, such as medical conferences focused on a specific therapeutic area or disease state as well as the Annual MSL Society Conference. Your goals for attending these events should include learning more about the MSL role, meeting those in the profession, and connecting with someone at a target company.

The following are ten essential steps for maximizing attendance during in-person networking events or conferences:

1. Dress professionally. Although it is acceptable to wear business casual to many conferences and networking events, you should always dress in business attire. Your appearance will contribute to your success in making a positive first impression on those you meet during events. For more information on appropriate business attire, see "What to Wear" in Chapter 7.

2. Prepare an icebreaker or brief introduction. Some aspiring MSLs may feel nervous about how to introduce themselves or how to initiate a conversation with other attendees at a conference or other networking event, especially with MSLs and MSL managers.

    Preparing and memorizing, in advance, a succinct, thirty-second introduction may help alleviate some of this anxiety. This brief introduction should include:

    • Information about yourself and your background (e.g., your full name; your academic background; PhD, PharmD, MD, etc.).

    • Your current role.

    • Highlights of your professional experience and accomplishments relevant to the MSL role.

    • Your purpose for attending the event, including the specific topics being covered that you are most interested in learning more about (not simply stating you want to become an MSL).

Practice this brief introduction multiple times in front of a mirror, which will enable you to identify inappropriate or awkward body language. Rehearse enough, so you are confident, comfortable, friendly, and conversational when introducing yourself.

3. Prepare relevant questions to ask MSLs or MSL managers. Asking appropriate questions and being able to effectively engage with MSLs and/or MSL managers during events will ensure you are able to gain valuable information, which will help you better prepare for interviews. Regardless of the questions you ask, always present yourself as friendly, respectful, enthusiastic, and appreciative. Appropriate questions to ask include:

- What specific skills or qualifications do you (or your manager) look for in an MSL applicant?
- What skills are most important to the success of an MSL?
- What is the hiring process at (their company)?
- What qualities do you (or their team) seek in candidates?
- How can someone strengthen their application with your company?
- Can I connect with you on LinkedIn after the conference/event?
- How can I set myself apart from others when applying for roles on your team?
- What is the best career advice you've ever received?
- What impresses you the most when you are reviewing or considering an MSL applicant?
- How did you break into your first MSL or MSL management role?

- What makes a CV stand out to you?
- What's your favorite tip for preparing for interviews?
- What's been one of your biggest career accomplishments?
- Do you have any favorite networking tips?
- What are some resources you would recommend to prepare for an MSL interview?
- Who else should I speak to at this event?
- What do you enjoy the most about your job?
- What advice would you have liked to have heard when you were starting out?
- What is one easily avoided mistake aspiring MSLs make when interviewing with you?
- What is one easily avoided mistake aspiring MSLs make when writing their CVs?
- What do MSLs on your team spend most of their time working on?
- How is the success of MSLs on your team measured?
- How do you think the MSL role will be different in five or ten years?
- What has changed the most about the MSL profession since you started?
- How do I address my lack of MSL experience when applying for roles?

4. Bring professional business cards. Business cards are beneficial because they enable you to immediately share your contact and professional details with those you meet during in-person events. If you don't have business cards, you can easily have them created using several online services.

When having your cards created, keep them simple and professional, and include the following information:

- Full name and academic credentials
- Mobile number
- Personal email address
- LinkedIn profile URL
- Possibly a professional photo (use the same photo from your LinkedIn profile for consistency)

5. Do not bring printed copies of your CV. The purpose of a conference or an in-person event is to network and possibly learn more about the MSL profession. If someone you meet during an event requests a copy of your CV, you can easily email them an electronic version of your CV (after obtaining their business card or contact details).

6. Correctly wear your name badge. If your name badge has a magnetic strip, a pin, or a clip on the back, it should be worn on the right side. Since most people are right-handed, when shaking hands during an introduction or a greeting, the other person will be able to read your name badge more easily. It's an easy, effective way to help those you meet remember your name.

7. Properly shake hands. When shaking hands, utilize the following gender-neutral techniques to make a positive impression:
   - Ensure your hand is clean (always bring hand sanitizer with you) and dry.
   - Use a single-handed shake (i.e., don't put your other hand on top of their hand).
   - When you extend your right hand, your palm faces left, not up or down.
   - Make full contact palm to palm (avoid merely grasping fingers).
   - Your grip should be firm and friendly.

- Hold for about two to three seconds.
- Maintain eye contact during the handshake.
- Exchange verbal introduction or greeting during the handshake.
- Smile.

8. Project professional body language. In addition to your appearance, your body language is also important in making a positive impression on those you meet during events. Part of this impression will be based on the manner in which you greet and engage with attendees. Utilize the following techniques when speaking with others at events:

   - Consistently make eye contact.
   - Smile when introducing yourself, as well as at other appropriate moments during a conversation.
   - Maintain an appropriate distance from others (don't stand or sit too closely).
   - Be aware of the volume of your voice (avoid speaking too loud or too soft).
   - Maintain an upright posture with your head up, shoulders back, and your arms unfolded at your sides.
   - Directly face the person with whom you are speaking.
   - Keep your upper arms close to your body, and avoid excessive gesturing with your hands.
   - Don't sway, rock, or pace when speaking.
   - Don't fidget.
   - Don't keep your hands in your pockets.
   - Avoid touching your face.

9. Make a positive impression. When speaking with other attendees, utilize the following techniques to ensure you make a positive impression on everyone you meet during events:

   • Be genuine and friendly.
   • Demonstrate enthusiasm.
   • Have a positive attitude.
   • Be confident yet humble.
   • Actively engage in conversation.
   • Be prepared to answer questions about your background and potential fit with the MSL career.
   • When responding to questions, keep your answers succinct (i.e., no more than 90 seconds); don't dominate the conversation.
   • Turn your mobile phone off or use the silent mode.
   • Don't be boring – it's not only about your science!

   At the end of a conversation, exchange business cards (if appropriate) and state something like, "It was nice meeting you," "I really enjoyed our conversation," or, "Thank you for sharing information about your company/team."

10. Follow up immediately. After meeting someone within the profession who may be able to help, immediately send a follow-up email and a LinkedIn connection request. In addition, if someone refers a name to you as a potential contact within the profession, send them an email (if you were provided their email address) and an invitation to connect on LinkedIn, and mention who recommended them as a contact. Refer to the "Thank-You Email Template and Content" section in "Chapter 6 for suggestions on what to include in the email.

5 Writing an Effective CV and Cover Letter

An effective MSL must be an excellent communicator. Your first opportunity to demonstrate your communication skills and relevant expertise—and your only form of initial communication with potential employers—will likely be through your *curriculum vitae* (CV, or "course of life" in Latin). This single piece of communication will determine if a hiring manager, recruiter, or someone from HR will be interested in you. All the effort you've put into researching the role and reviewing job descriptions will not make any difference if you don't get this part right. A well-written CV creates an immediate but lasting positive impression, whereas a poorly constructed CV will likely prevent you from being considered or ever being granted an interview.

There are essential elements that an MSL CV must include to be considered by HR or the hiring manager. These essential elements include utilizing appropriate keywords, specific formatting, listing relevant accomplishments, and matching your CV to the job description of the MSL role for which you are applying.

As with most hiring managers, I could quickly assess if an applicant was a potential match. Most of the CVs I have received and reviewed over the years were easy to eliminate due to three primary reasons:

1. Lack of experience in the relevant therapeutic area or disease state
2. Lack of appropriate educational level (i.e., a doctorate degree)
3. Lack of relevant skills

Most of the time, the hiring manager will not consider a CV unless one of these criteria, a combination of these criteria, or all three of these criteria are met, simply because the hiring manager does not feel there is a potential fit or because executive management has decided that one, a combination of, or all three are minimum requirements for the role. Although the lack of all three of these criteria could result in your CV being easily eliminated, the single most important detail I looked for when reviewing a candidate's CV was whether they had relevant therapeutic, disease state, or drug indication experience.

If you do not have relevant therapeutic area experience when applying for a role, you are completely wasting your time submitting your CV, and I can almost guarantee it will be discarded as not qualified. If I did not see any relevance to the approved drug indication, disease state, or therapeutic area for which I had an opening, I would stop reviewing that applicant. In fact, this is essential to most MSL managers, and a study revealed that 62 percent of U.S.-based MSL managers and 54 percent of MSL managers globally reported that "relevant therapeutic area/disease state experience" is the most relevant/important information on a CV/resume for an MSL position (Tables 45 and 46).

Table 45

Survey question: "Typically, what do you think is the most relevant/important information on a CV/resume for an MSL position? (Please check all that apply.)"

Most Relevant Information on an MSL CV			
Relevant therapeutic area and/or disease state	99%	Lives within region; no need to relocate	66%
Work history	98%	Previous companies worked for	59%
Prior MSL experience	98%	Has existing KOL relationships to leverage immediately	59%
Prior MSL experience within the same therapeutic area and/or disease state	92%	Relevant accomplishments	54%
Demonstrated communication skills	92%	Leadership skills	51%
Demonstrated ability to build KOL relationships	79%	Other soft skills	20%
Industry experience	77%	Other (please specify)	18%
Clinical research experience or clinical expertise	72%	Relevant publications	13%
Academic background (i.e., confirming they have a doctorate degree or appropriate background)	71%		

2018 "MSL Hiring Practices Survey," MSL Society
97 MSL Managers
U.S. Results

Table 46
Survey question: "Typically, what do you think is the most relevant/important information on a CV/resume for an MSL position? (Please check all that apply.)"

Most Relevant Information on an MSL CV			
Demonstrated ability to build KOL relationships	59%	Lives within region; no need to relocate	34%
Work history	58%	Leadership skills	28%
Prior MSL experience	55%	Has existing KOL relationships to leverage immediately	28%
Relevant therapeutic area and/or disease state experience	54%	Previous companies worked for	28%
Demonstrated ability to build KOL relationships	53%	Other soft skills	28%
Academic background (i.e., confirming they have a doctorate degree or appropriate background)	52%	Relevant accomplishments	27%
Prior MSL experience within the same therapeutic area and/or disease state	46%	Relevant publications	7%
Industry experience	46%	Other (please specify)	4%
Clinical research experience or clinical expertise	39%		

2018 "MSL Hiring Practices Survey," MSL Society
185 MSL Managers
Global Results

Another primary reason that an applicant's CV is easily eliminated is a lack of appropriate educational level (i.e., a doctorate degree). As mentioned in Chapter 2, a doctorate degree is the academic standard for the MSL profession, both in the U.S. and globally. Although not having a doctorate degree doesn't mean it will be impossible to break into the MSL profession, it will be much more difficult because applicants with doctorate degrees are typically preferred. While there are a limited number of MSL roles that do not require a doctorate degree, these are increasingly rare. Therefore, if you decide to pursue an MSL career without having a doctorate degree (especially in the U.S.), it will be even more critical to thoroughly research target companies and roles and apply only to positions for which you are an absolute match based on the job description.

Finally, a lack of relevant skills is another primary reason an MSL applicant's CV will be quickly eliminated. Regardless of whether you are submitting your CV online to the company website or to a recruiter, there is limited flexibility in what will be considered if you do not meet the minimum requirements for the role. The simplest way to avoid being immediately eliminated and wasting your time when submitting your CV is to read the job description thoroughly and apply only to roles that match well with your professional background, disease state or therapeutic area experience, and skills.

In the remainder of this chapter, you will learn what specific details and information MSL hiring managers look for and expect when reviewing a CV. I will provide specific recommendations on what to include in your CV, as well as what mistakes to avoid. Collectively, this information will help your CV receive more than a cursory review and move you one step closer to landing your first MSL role. Lastly, I will also provide templates for both a successful CV and cover letter.

In the MSL Profession, the CV Is Considered the Standard

"Resume" and "CV" are often used interchangeably within MSL job descriptions, but by definition, there are differences between them that determine their usage.

A resume is typically one to two pages and summarizes your skills, education, and career. It's used when applying for most general job openings. In contrast, a CV is typically multiple pages that consist of a more detailed summary of your skills, education, and career, as well as other areas, such as professional affiliations, publications, and presentations. A CV is used when applying for most academic, research, scientific, and MSL roles.

Although you may encounter both terms when discussing the role with recruiters or others in the industry or when reviewing MSL job descriptions, the longer CV is the expected format when applying for MSL roles. In my experience as a hiring manager, I never seriously considered a candidate who submitted a one-page resume or CV. Whenever I saw an abbreviated resume or CV, I always thought something was missing, and my immediate impression was that the applicant did not have the proper experience or background. As a result, I determined they were likely not a good match for the role I was hiring for. Regardless of whether you refer to this document as a resume or a CV, the expectation among MSL hiring managers is that MSL applicants will submit a CV that is longer than one page. In fact, a study revealed that 69 percent of MSL managers globally and 59 percent of U.S.-based MSL managers reported that the appropriate length of an MSL CV/resume is between two and three pages (Tables 47 and 48).

Table 47
Survey question: "What is the appropriate length for an MSL CV/resume?"

Appropriate Length of CV/Resume	
1 page	2%
2 pages	43%
3 pages	26%
4 pages	9%
5 pages	1%
5+ pages	1%
I have no preference	20%

2018 "MSL Hiring Practices Survey," MSL Society
185 MSL Managers
Global Results

Table 48
Survey question: "What is the appropriate length for an MSL CV/resume?"

Appropriate Length of CV/Resume	
1 page	0%
2 pages	32%
3 pages	27%
4 pages	10%
5 pages	1%
5+ pages	0%
I have no preference	30%

2018 "MSL Hiring Practices Survey," MSL Society
97 MSL Managers
U.S. Results

Use the Chronological Format for Your CV

The two methods for displaying information on a CV include the chronological and functional formats. A *functional* format uses categories and lists your skills and accomplishments in their order of importance. Functional CVs are typically used for those with limited career histories or those looking to make a career transition. Although you are making a career transition into the MSL role, do not use the functional format as it will not list your skills and qualifications in the expected format.

The standard CV format for MSL roles is the *chronological* format. As the name implies, the chronological format demonstrates a progression and timeline of your career, starting with the most recent role. The primary distinction is that with a chronological format, your job responsibilities and accomplishments are placed under your title, the company name, and dates of employment. A chronologically formatted CV that displays a logical career progression and includes your relevant experience, skills, and knowledge demonstrates to MSL managers how your career has prepared you for the MSL role.

Match Your MSL CV to an Employer's Needs

Your CV needs to grab the reader's attention quickly. MSL managers will review numerous CVs for every single MSL vacancy.

To get your CV noticed, it must be targeted toward the *employer's* needs. To accomplish this, it's crucial that you customize and match your CV, including relevant skills and accomplishments (as much as possible), to the needs of the role listed in the job description. As a result, you will need to customize your CV for every MSL role for which you apply.

When I received a CV, I typically spent less than one minute conducting an initial review. Most hiring managers will also conduct a quick initial review as well. In fact, 59 percent of MSL managers both globally and in the U.S. reported they spend less than three minutes on an initial CV/resume review (Tables 49 and 50).

Table 49
Survey question: "On average, how much time do you spend reviewing a CV/resume the very first time you review it (aka 'first pass')?"

Average CV Review Time	
5 seconds or less	1%
15 seconds or less	1%
30 seconds or less	10%
1 minute or less	13%
1 - 3 minutes	34%
3 - 5 minutes	23%
5 - 10 minutes	15%
10+ minutes	4%

2018 "MSL Hiring Practices Survey," MSL Society
185 MSL Managers
Global Results

Table 50
Survey question: "On average, how much time do you spend reviewing a CV/Resume the very first time you review it (aka 'first pass')?"

Average CV Review Time	
5 seconds or less	0%
15 seconds or less	1%
30 seconds or less	13%
1 minute or less	15%
1 - 3 minutes	30%
3 - 5 minutes	24%
5 - 10 minutes	13%
10+ minutes	3%

2018 "MSL Hiring Practices Survey," MSL Society
97 MSL Managers
U.S. Results

As a result of the quick initial review conducted by most managers, do not use long, complex sentences. Instead, use keywords in a bullet-point format as much as possible. This will enable the hiring manager and others reviewing your CV to quickly scan for key pieces of relevant information.

Be specific when listing your accomplishments. Incorporate details regarding not only actual tasks performed, but also what you achieved in each of your prior work experiences. For example, list any presentations you gave at scientific meetings or congresses that are directly related to the role for which you are applying.

Wherever possible, quantify your impact with statistics such as percentages or numbers. Statistics are easy to interpret, and they make an impact. They demonstrate to hiring managers what you could potentially contribute to their team and the company.

Do not include links to personal social media profiles other than your LinkedIn profile. Again, your LinkedIn profile should be well written and include sections describing your accomplishments that are most relevant to the MSL role.

Do not embellish any prior work experience or academic achievements. Doing so will result in your application being eliminated because any discrepancies will be easily discovered. Most companies perform thorough, routine background checks to verify key information on your application. Many companies will also utilize simple online searches, including social media, to verify information.

The Importance of Keywords in Your CV

When you submit your CV and application materials on a pharmaceutical, biotechnology, or medical device company website, your CV may be initially reviewed by an internal recruiter, someone in HR, a hiring manager, or it may be entered into applicant tracking software (ATS). Assume your CV will be scanned by an applicant tracking system.

Applicant tracking software is designed to prescreen and search an applicant's CV for specific relevant keywords that match those from the MSL job description. It also serves to eliminate unqualified candidates.

The software will match and retain only those CVs that contain the predetermined keywords identified for that role and will discard the remaining unrelated or unmatched CVs. As a result, it's essential to utilize relevant keywords from the job description throughout your CV to prevent it from being eliminated from consideration by the ATS.

The following are three strategies for utilizing keywords to get past the initial automated screening process. Incorporating these strategies will increase the chances your CV will be reviewed by the hiring manager, someone from HR, or a recruiter.

1. Embed keywords from the job description. In most cases, many of the keywords that an ATS has predetermined for a role are those listed in the responsibilities of the role in the job

description. For example, if the job description requires that candidates have experience in "developing and managing KOL relationships" within the cardiovascular therapeutic area, then each of these words should be embedded in your CV. To become more familiar with the keywords utilized in MSL job descriptions, you should review multiple MSL job descriptions in your therapeutic area or disease state. Another tactic is to search and review LinkedIn MSL profiles within your therapeutic area to familiarize yourself with common keywords used.

2. Incorporate the most relevant keywords. Highlight your experiences using keywords that match the job description. Focus on what you have accomplished in your career to date and highlight those experiences that match the keywords and the needs of the role from the job description for each MSL role for which you apply. All company types (e.g., pharma, biotechnology, medical device, etc.) are utilizing applicant tracking software in their recruiting processes. As a result, ensure you incorporate the most relevant keywords that match the needs of the role into every CV you submit.

3. Utilize keywords throughout the document. Don't simply list keywords. While including a "therapeutic area" section in your CV is an important method to ensure relevant keywords are included, a list by itself is usually not sufficient to get noticed by the tracking software. Many applicant tracking software systems scan for the frequency of keywords spread throughout the entire document, rather than simply a list of keywords. For example, if the job description states that "building and maintaining effective relationships" is important for the role, a statement in your CV such as "built and maintained a relationship with one of the leading KOLs in X (whatever your therapeutic area may be) while a researcher at the University of X (whatever institution)" might

capture the attention of the hiring manager. This type of statement may also effectively incorporate some of the keywords that the applicant tracking software has predetermined for the role. While it's important to embed relevant keywords throughout your CV for the purposes of trying to avoid being eliminated by an ATS, it's equally important to ensure your CV has the expected elements that will make it legible and easy to review by a hiring manager, someone from HR, or a recruiter. These elements include an easily readable font style, font size, overall layout (e.g., use of whitespace, category headings, etc.), and correct spelling and grammar.

Proper Format and What to Include in Your CV

Over the course of my career, in numerous countries, I have seen CVs presented in several different formats. In some countries, the expected format may change because additional information is expected and often requested, such as date of birth or a photo. As a result, it's important to be aware of and adhere to the expected format in your country or region. However, the preferred format of most MSL managers (which can be used in most countries) is the following template. What follows also includes specific guidelines and numerous suggested do's and don'ts on what to include in each section of your CV. Utilizing this CV format will enable you to effectively highlight your relevant skills, experience, and therapeutic area or disease state expertise so that your CV reads like a qualified MSL applicant. Using the following suggestions will also increase the chance your CV will be flagged for review by the applicant tracking software when submitting your application.

MSL CV Template

Your Name, Academic Credentials

Home City
Personal Email Address
Mobile Number
LinkedIn Profile URL

Career Objective

Therapeutic Area/Disease State/Clinical Experience:

•

Key Achievements

•

Education

Degree   Title   Year Achieved

Institution

Professional Experience

Job Title   Start Year–End Year

Company/Institution Name

Responsibilities

•

Accomplishments

•

Professional Societies and Associations: (only if relevant)

Organization Name   Years of Membership

Publications: (only if relevant)

Publications relevant to the specific MSL role for which you are applying

Title, Month/Year

Your name ~ CV
(footer on each page)

General Guidelines for Formatting Your CV

Prior to submitting your CV online, be aware that some company websites will specify which file format is required for resume/CV submission within their system (e.g., .doc, .docx, .pdf). However, when possible, always submit your CV as a PDF to preserve formatting. This is important because a PDF is an image file, and a Word document is a text file; as a result, what seems like a well-formatted Word document CV on your computer may look very different when hiring managers reviews it on their computers. You should also incorporate the following general guidelines when formatting your CV:

- ✓ Use a professional font style, such as Arial, Calibri, or Verdana.
- ✓ Use 12-point font for ease of reading.
- ✓ Use standard black text color.
- ✓ Use bullet points for key information.
- ✓ Proofread it for spelling and grammatical errors.
- ✓ Create your CV in Microsoft Word format (.doc or .docx).
- ✓ When saving your CV, use your full name as the file name (e.g., "Dr. John Smith-CV.pdf" or "Dr. John Smith-CV.doc").
- ✓ Include your full name in the footer section on each page (e.g., "Your name ~ CV").

Contact Information

It is important that your CV is accurate and has your full name and contact details listed across the top of the document.

Do:

- ✓ Your first and last name followed by the academic credentials of the highest degree you have earned (e.g., PharmD, PhD, MD, etc.)

✓ Your home city (street address is not necessary)
✓ Your personal email address
✓ Your mobile number
✓ Your LinkedIn profile URL

Don't:

✓ Use an unprofessional email address, such as awesomemsl@gmail.com

Career Objective Statement

The first section is the "Career Objective", and it is your first opportunity to match your CV to the needs of the MSL role for which you are applying.

Do:

✓ Use one or two sentences that emphasize how your expertise and experience match the needs of the specific MSL role.
✓ Create an attention-grabbing statement by incorporating relevant keywords used in the job description.
✓ Include quantifiable industry-specific accomplishments.
✓ Make your objective specific to each specific MSL role for which you are applying.
✓ Use a bullet format.

Don't:

✓ Focus this section on what you want; instead, focus on what the company needs.
✓ Use long sentences.
✓ Have any spelling or grammatical errors.

Therapeutic Area/Disease State/Clinical Experience

The most important section on your CV and opportunity to demonstrate how your background matches the needs of the role for which you are applying is the "Therapeutic Area/Disease State/Clinical

Experience" section. Recall that according to a global survey, 62 percent of U.S.-based MSL managers and 54 percent of MSL managers globally reported that "relevant therapeutic area/disease state experience" is the most relevant and important information on a CV/resume for an MSL position.

Do:

✓ Include only therapeutic area/disease state/clinical experience relevant to the specific MSL role for which you are applying.

✓ Use the exact keywords or terms that are used in the job description. For example, if the job description uses the word "oncology," you should use the word "oncology" on your CV, not "cancer."

✓ If you have experience in multiple therapeutic areas or disease states, you can list them in this section, but place the most relevant ones at the top of the list.

✓ Use a bullet format.

Don't:

✓ List every therapeutic area or disease state in which you have experience (if you have experience in multiple areas). Limit this list to four or five relevant therapeutic areas/disease states.

✓ Use long sentences.

✓ Have any spelling or grammatical errors.

Key Achievements

The "Key Achievements" section is an opportunity to highlight your most relevant accomplishments that are directly related to the MSL role for which you are applying.

Do:

✓ Keep it short; limit your list to five relevant key achievements.

✓ Include the achievements that will likely have the biggest impact. However, only include achievements that are the most relevant to the MSL role for which you are applying (for example, presentations given at a scientific conference focusing on the same therapeutic area or disease state).

✓ Only list the top two to three relevant presentations you have given that are directly related to the specific therapeutic area or disease state for the MSL role for which you are applying.

✓ Use metrics to demonstrate results (e.g., number of attendees during your presentation).

✓ Use a bullet format.

Don't:

✓ Lie or exaggerate.

✓ List irrelevant presentations.

✓ List presentations that are not career related.

✓ Use long sentences.

✓ Have any spelling or grammatical errors.

Education, Licenses, and Certificates

This section is one of the first sections of your CV that hiring managers will typically review. As mentioned, most MSL managers prefer applicants with a doctorate degree, so MSL hiring managers (and possibly others at a company) will verify you have the expected education.

Do:

✓ List all degrees and all relevant certificates or licenses (e.g., licensed pharmacist) in reverse chronological order, starting with the most recently earned.

✓ Include the degree title, name of school and location, and year of graduation or completion.

Don't:

✓ Include irrelevant degrees like an associate's degree or certificates that are not related to the MSL role or the pharmaceutical industry.

✓ Lie about having completed a degree, dates of attendance, or any other detail.

✓ Include subheadings such as relevant coursework, majors, honors and awards, clinical labs, academic advisors, dissertation committee members, etc.

✓ List grade point averages.

✓ Have any spelling or grammatical errors.

Professional Experience

It's crucial that your professional experience matches the manager's needs for the MSL role for which they are hiring.

Do:

✓ List the full title, start and end year, and the full name of the company or institution for each role.

✓ Provide a comprehensive overview of your career history, starting with the most recent role and continuing in reverse chronological order.

✓ Include relevant internships or volunteer positions.

✓ Use bullets to list information.

✓ Use metrics to demonstrate results.

✓ Use action verbs to highlight relevant experiences.

✓ Use language specific to the MSL role, such as keywords from the job description for the role for which you are applying.

✓ Create separate sections for responsibilities and accomplishments.

- ✓ Under the responsibilities section, highlight the activities for each of your previous roles that are most relevant to the MSL role for which you are applying.
- ✓ Under the responsibilities section, list specific, relevant projects you have worked on that are directly related to the therapeutic area or specific skills listed in the MSL job description for the role for which you are applying.
- ✓ Under the accomplishments section, list awards received and recognition from colleagues or management that are most relevant to the MSL role.
- ✓ Under the accomplishments section, list all relevant presentations you have given (that were not included in the "Key Achievement" section) which are directly related to the specific therapeutic area or disease state for the MSL role for which you are applying.

Don't:
- ✓ Write a summary of your job description for each role.
- ✓ Mention every responsibility or accomplishment.
- ✓ Include presentations that are not career related.
- ✓ Lie or exaggerate about the title of a role or responsibilities.
- ✓ Lie about or exaggerate the dates of employment.
- ✓ Have any spelling or grammatical errors.

Professional Societies and Associations (only if relevant)

Another opportunity to highlight relevant areas of experience that match the needs of the MSL job description is the "Professional Societies and Associations" section. However, only include this section on your CV if you are a member of relevant professional societies or associations.

Do:

✓ Include the full name and years of membership for professional or medical societies and associations of which you are a member.

✓ Include those that are relevant to the therapeutic area or disease state for the role for which you are applying or, more broadly, those relevant to the pharmaceutical, biotechnology, or healthcare industries; a particular disease; or a scientific area.

✓ Mention if you served in a leadership role (e.g., served on a panel, served on a committee, etc.).

Don't:

✓ List religious or social clubs.

✓ List more than five organizations.

Publications (only if relevant)

It's important to be selective when considering which publications to include in your CV. Although it may seem counterintuitive, do not list every publication in which you were an author. Only list publications that are directly related to the MSL role for which you are applying. Doing so will further highlight your experience in a specific therapeutic area or disease state. Including irrelevant publications simply highlights you are a recognized published expert in something unrelated to what the manager is hiring for. However, only include this section on your CV if you have relevant publications.

Do:

✓ For each publication, include the full article title, journal or source name, and year of publication.

✓ List publications that are relevant to the disease state, drug indication, or therapeutic area for the MSL role for which you are applying.

Don't:

- ✓ List publications that are unrelated to the therapeutic area or disease state for the MSL role for which you are applying.
- ✓ List more than seven relevant publications.

The Importance of Your Cover Letter and Making First Contact

The most important document a hiring manager considers when reviewing an applicant is their CV. However, a cover letter can be an effective way to further highlight your relevant experience and your therapeutic area and disease state expertise. It also enables you to express your desire for a role and to demonstrate your personality. A cover letter may help you distinguish yourself when several potential candidates are being considered. However, be aware that only about half of MSL managers (both globally and in the U.S.) read and place high importance on cover letters (Tables 51 and 52).

Table 51
Survey question: "Typically, I read all cover letters and place a high importance on them."

Read All Cover Letters	
Agree	47%
Disagree	53%

2018 "MSL Hiring Practices Survey," MSL Society
97 MSL Managers
U.S. Results

Table 52
Survey question: "Typically, I read all cover letters and place a high importance on them."

Read All Cover Letters	
Agree	54%
Disagree	46%

2018 "MSL Hiring Practices Survey," MSL Society
185 MSL Managers
Global Results

If you decide to utilize a cover letter when sending an email to a recruiter or anyone working for a company, always incorporate the cover letter within the body of the email and include your CV as an attachment. If you send both your cover letter and CV as attachments, you risk the chance that the recipient will only read your CV. This may be your only communication before someone determines if you are a potential fit for the role, so incorporating your cover letter within the body of the email increases the chance it will be read.

However, as mentioned, it's crucial to your success to only apply for roles for which your background matches the specific requirements of the role. Typically, both hiring managers and internal recruiters will only consider applicants with specific backgrounds that match the needs of the role as defined within the job description. Furthermore, it's also important to be aware that external recruiters are hired by companies to find candidates with specific backgrounds and will not submit anyone who does not meet the requirements specified by the company. If you apply for roles that do not match your background, you are highly unlikely to get a positive response to your application, and it will likely be rejected.

Guidelines for Formatting Your Cover Letter

In addition to incorporating your cover letter directly within the body of the email, the following are a few additional formatting suggestions:

- ✓ In the subject line, specify the MSL role for which you are applying.
- ✓ Use a professional font style such as Arial, Calibri, or Verdana.
- ✓ Use 12-point font for ease of reading.
- ✓ Use standard black text color.
- ✓ Use bullet points for key information.
- ✓ Limit the letter to three short paragraphs of three to five sentences for each paragraph.
- ✓ Proofread for spelling and grammatical errors before sending.
- ✓ Attach your CV in PDF format.

Cover Letter Template and Content

The following is a cover letter template along with several suggested do's and don'ts on what to include. It's important to keep it brief and relevant. Use a maximum of two or three paragraphs, including bullets, rather than one large block of text. Throughout your cover letter, highlight how your skills and experience match the requirements of the role listed in the job description. Always send a unique cover letter specific to each MSL role and include the following sections:

Salutation

Do:
- ✓ Ensure that each cover letter is personalized and addressed to a specific individual.
- ✓ Use appropriate titles such as Dr., Mr., Mrs., or Ms.

Don't:

✓ Misspell the recipient's name... ever!

✓ Use generic salutations such as, "To whom it may concern," "Dear Sir," or "Dear Madam."

First, Middle, and Final Paragraphs

Do:

✓ First paragraph:
- Introduce yourself.
- Mention the specific role for which you are applying.
- Describe how your experience fits with the needs of the role.
- Specify how your related experiences will enable you to be successful in the role.
- Ensure there is a clear transition to subsequent paragraphs.

✓ Middle paragraph:
- Highlight how you are a match for the role.
- Highlight specific accomplishments or experiences using keywords from the job description.
- When possible, use a few sentences from a recommendation that highlights your potential fit with the role.
- When possible, mention relevant connections with the company, hiring manager, or mutual colleagues.
- Incorporate company-specific details highlighting your knowledge of the company.

✓ Final paragraph:
- Direct the reader to your attached CV.
- Request an interview.
- Thank the person for his or her time and consideration.

Don't:
- ✓ Restate your CV.
- ✓ Mention salary requirements (unless specifically requested).
- ✓ Send with any typos, spelling, or grammatical errors.
- ✓ Send your cover letter without your CV.
- ✓ Provide information that is not relevant to the MSL role.

Close

When concluding a cover letter, it's important to utilize professional language.

Do:
- ✓ Use business neutral terms such as "Regards," "Respectfully," or, "Thanks."
- ✓ Keep it simple.

Don't:
- ✓ Use religious terms such as "God Bless" or "God Be with You."
- ✓ Use personal terms such as "Yours Truly" or "Warm Regards."

Signature

Ensure the signature section contains your complete contact details.

Do:
- ✓ Use your full name.
- ✓ Add your LinkedIn profile URL.
- ✓ Include your email address.
- ✓ List your mobile phone number.

Don't:
- ✓ Forget to include your academic credentials (PhD, PharmD, MD, etc.).

✓ Use a font style or size that is different from the body of the cover letter.

✓ Include quotes (religious, motivational, etc.).

Responding to a Phone Interview Request

If, after reviewing your cover letter and CV, an external recruiter or an individual at a company feels you are a potential fit for the role, they will send an email to arrange a mutually convenient time to speak. The purpose of this first conversation—referred to as a phone screen—is to learn more about your experience, discuss the role, evaluate your communication skills, and ultimately determine if you will move forward in the interview process.

Typically, you will be given a few different options for dates and times. When replying to the email, keep your response succinct, do not alter the original message or subject line, and before agreeing to a date and time, ensure you:

✓ Account for any time-zone differences.

✓ Have no schedule conflicts.

✓ Give yourself adequate time to prepare.

If You Do Not Get a Response

Although there may be a number of reasons you don't get a response to your application materials, including the role has been put on hold, or an internal candidate has been identified, the most likely reason is it was determined you were not a match for the role. HR departments and recruiters receive numerous applications for each posted MSL role and typically only respond to applicants they determine are a match for each specific role.

If you have not received a response after sending your CV and cover letter, it is acceptable and appropriate to send a follow-up email. However, be sure to wait a minimum of two weeks before following up. When sending a follow-up email:

✓ Never be unprofessional.

✓ Never send more than one follow-up email.

✓ Never call to inquire about your application.

If you do not receive a response to this follow-up message, you should assume the company determined you were not a match for that particular role.

Part 3

The MSL Hiring Process

6

The Phone Screen and Phone Interview

The Phone Screen

If, after applying for a role, it is determined you are a potential fit, an external recruiter or someone working directly for the company to which you have applied will send an email to arrange a mutually convenient time to speak. This first conversation is typically referred to as a phone screen. You should be prepared to participate in the phone screen virtually using Zoom, Skype, Webex, Microsoft Teams, or other similar software because companies are increasingly using these as alternatives to the traditional phone screen. For several detailed techniques and best practices regarding how to successfully prepare for a virtual interview, see Appendix B.

The purpose of the phone screen is to learn more about your relevant experiences, discuss the role, assess your interest, evaluate your communication skills, and ultimately determine if you will move forward in the interview process. Because companies and recruiters receive numerous applications for each open MSL position, both utilize the phone screen as a cost-efficient, time-saving method to narrow down the number of potential candidates.

However, you should use the phone screen as an opportunity to learn more about the role and the company. During the phone screen, the interviewer will:

✓ Clarify and discuss details on your CV.

✓ Verify that your answers are consistent with your CV.

✓ Compare your past experiences with the needs of the MSL role.

✓ Determine if you have the right qualifications.

✓ Assess your personality fit with the company.

✓ Evaluate your communication skills.

✓ Clarify your understanding of the responsibilities of the MSL role.

✓ Evaluate your enthusiasm for and interest in the role.

✓ Possibly discuss your salary expectations (never bring up salary first!).

✓ Discuss relocation (if necessary).

✓ Discuss next steps in the hiring process.

What to Expect During a Phone Screen

Generally, the phone screen will begin with the interviewer providing some background information about the specific MSL role and how it fits within the structure of the company.

Typically, the interviewer will then ask you to review your CV and will ask you a number of questions. Although the interviewer will ask specific questions about your experiences and qualifications, they likely will not evaluate your scientific background since that will be a primary focus of the phone interview with the hiring manager.

In fact, the interviewer conducting the phone screen likely will not have a scientific background. However, during the phone screen, you should emphasize how your scientific background matches the needs of the role without discussing specific details.

The final few minutes of the phone screen are usually set aside to provide you with an opportunity to ask questions. Although this is the general format for the phone screen, there are a few differences when speaking with someone directly at a pharmaceutical or medical device company versus an external recruiter.

Speaking with Someone Directly Connected to a Pharmaceutical, Biotechnology, Medical Device, or Other Healthcare Company

If the initial call is with a representative from the company, it will typically be brief, lasting from fifteen to twenty minutes. However, you should be prepared to speak for a minimum of thirty minutes. This call may be directly with someone in HR, an internal recruiter who works at the company, or an external contractor who is hired by the company. The interviewer will quickly assess your background and provide a short description of the role. You will be asked a number of questions about your relevant experiences, possibly your salary requirements, and, if applicable, whether you are open to relocation.

Speaking with an External Recruiter

If the initial call is with an external recruiter, the length of the call is generally longer, lasting from thirty to forty-five minutes. However, you should be prepared to speak for a minimum of one hour. As a result, there will be a more detailed discussion about how your academic background and related therapeutic area experience match the needs of the role for which you are applying.

Regardless if the phone screen is with someone working directly for the company or an external recruiter, the primary purpose of this initial conversation will be to determine if there is an initial match between your background and the specific needs of the role. Ultimately, the interviewer will determine if you will be selected for a phone interview with the hiring manager, which is the next step in the hiring process.

To gain a greater understanding of the important differences between an internal and external recruiter, see Appendix C.

Strategies for a Successful Phone Screen

Success during a phone screen will be based primarily on your preparation and communication skills during the call. Regardless of whether you will be speaking with someone directly with the company or an external recruiter, the following are a number of recommendations to help you prepare for the phone screen.

Before the Call

If you will be speaking with someone working directly for a pharmaceutical or medical device company, it's critical to research the company and the product(s) the MSL will support using the techniques described in Chapter 3. However, be aware that if you will be speaking with an external recruiter during the phone screen, you may not know the name of the pharmaceutical or medical device company prior to the call.

A survey conducted by the MSL Society highlights the importance of researching the company and its products prior to an interview. This study revealed that 93 percent of current MSLs in the U.S. and 89 percent of MSLs globally reported that they "always" research the company when interviewing for an MSL role. This same study also found that 94 percent of current MSLs in the U.S. and 89 percent of MSLs globally "always" research the company's product(s) or drugs in development when interviewing for an MSL role (Tables 53–56).

Table 53

Survey question: "When preparing for an interview: How often do you research the company when interviewing for an MSL role?"

Frequency: Researching Company	
Always	93%
Often	6%
Sometimes	1%
Rarely	<1%
Never	0%

2018 "MSL Hiring Practices Survey," MSL Society
303 MSLs (or equivalent title)
U.S. Results

Table 54

Survey question: "When preparing for an interview: How often do you research the company when interviewing for an MSL role?"

Frequency: Researching Company	
Always	89%
Often	8%
Sometimes	2%
Rarely	<1%
Never	1%

2018 "MSL Hiring Practices Survey," MSL Society
545 MSLs (or equivalent title)
Global Results

Table 55
Survey question: "When preparing for an interview: How often do you research the company's product(s) or drugs in development ('pipeline') that the MSL position supports when interviewing for an MSL role?"

Frequency: Pipeline Research	
Always	94%
Often	4%
Sometimes	1%
Rarely	1%
Never	<1%

2018 "MSL Hiring Practices Survey," MSL Society
303 MSLs (or equivalent title)
U.S. Results

Table 56
Survey question: "When preparing for an interview: How often do you research the company's product(s) or drugs in development ('pipeline') that the MSL position supports when interviewing for an MSL role?"

Frequency: Pipeline Research	
Always	89%
Often	7%
Sometimes	2%
Rarely	1%
Never	<1%

2018 "MSL Hiring Practices Survey," MSL Society
545 MSLs (or equivalent title)
Global Results

In addition to conducting research, review your CV thoroughly, and ensure you know every detail. Most interviewers will use your CV as a basis for their questions during the call, so be prepared to answer any question regarding the information on your CV. Listen carefully to every question you are asked throughout the interview. Respond to each question enthusiastically with confident, succinct, fact-filled responses limited to 90 seconds.

Prior to the phone screen, it's also important to establish a professional environment conducive to an interview. The following are several best practices for creating a professional environment:

- ✓ Set up a professional greeting on your voicemail by speaking your full name in a clear manner.
- ✓ Organize a quiet area without distracting background noises (e.g., children, pets, music, television, etc.).
- ✓ Have enough space to be able to get up and walk around during the call to raise your energy level.
- ✓ If you plan to use a mobile phone, ensure there is clear coverage.
- ✓ Ideally, have an earpiece or headset for your phone.

Finally, the following are several recommendations for preparing for the phone screen:

- ✓ Have a printed copy of your CV in front of you. However, the exception to this is if the interview is being conducted virtually on camera utilizing Zoom, Skype, Webex, Microsoft Teams, or other similar technology where the interviewer will be able to see you. During a virtual interview, having printed material in front of you can be distracting and make you appear unprepared.
- ✓ Be prepared to discuss every detail of your CV. The interviewer will use your CV as a basis for their questions.
- ✓ Research the company, including reviewing their website, to ensure you are thoroughly familiar with the product(s) the MSL team supports.
- ✓ Be prepared to highlight how your background is a match to the needs of the role.
- ✓ Practice succinct answers to the traditional type questions that may be asked. A description and specific questions are outlined later in this chapter.

✓ Review the "Behavioral Type Questions" section later in this chapter to successfully prepare for this type of question (although these are not typically asked during the phone screen).

✓ Be prepared with a response if asked about a perceived weakness. Provide examples of how you have addressed the weakness and have already improved.

✓ Be able to address your lack of MSL experience with succinct examples of accomplishments and skills relevant to the role as well as the value you will bring to the team.

✓ Plan to take notes of important information for reference when preparing for the phone interview with the hiring manager.

✓ Prepare a number of questions to ask the interviewer. Suggested questions are included later in this chapter.

✓ Be prepared to speak at least fifteen minutes before the call is scheduled to begin.

During the Call

During the phone screen, it is important to be professional and communicate clearly.

✓ Smile, be friendly, and have a positive attitude.

✓ Express enthusiasm for and interest in the role and company.

✓ When reviewing your CV, never read from it.

✓ Don't ever ask to skip a question, and keep your responses succinct.

✓ Sit up straight to clearly project your voice.

✓ Use verbal cues, such as "I see" and "I understand," to indicate you are following the conversation.

✓ Pay attention to the volume and pace of your voice to ensure it's appropriate.

✓ Occasionally confirm you have completely answered a question with a response such as, "Did I answer your question?"

✓ When responding to questions, answer only the question asked; do not deviate into unrelated topics.

✓ Avoid rambling when responding to questions by limiting your answers to 90 seconds and pausing to allow the hiring manager to interject comments or questions.

✓ Interject relevant questions, as appropriate, throughout the call to gain a better understanding of the role, as well as the company.

✓ Be sure to mention any relevant experiences that are not on your CV or any that have not been discussed.

✓ Never mislead or misrepresent anything regarding your background or experience.

✓ Take notes to capture key points; however, note-taking should not distract you from engaging in the conversation or from actively listening. However, if the interview is being conducted virtually on camera and visible to the interviewer, be sure to inform them that you will be taking notes on important points being discussed.

✓ Demonstrate your knowledge of the role, the company, and the product(s) the MSL team supports.

✓ Discuss generally how your scientific background, knowledge, skills, and accomplishments will have an immediate, positive impact on the MSL team.

✓ Occasionally stand to convey confidence and to project your voice in a professional manner.

✓ Enunciate and speak clearly when responding to questions.

✓ Inform the interviewer if you have a poor phone connection or are having difficulty hearing them.

✓ Never initiate a discussion regarding salary or benefits. Refer to Chapter 8 for guidelines on how to address questions related to salary and benefits expectations.

Questions You May Be Asked During a Phone Screen

Interviewers do not typically ask behavioral questions utilizing the STAR (situation, task, action, result) method during a phone screen; however, they will likely be utilized during the phone or in-person interviews.

What follows are typical questions you may be asked during a phone screen. Remember to listen to each question carefully and respond enthusiastically with confident, succinct, fact-filled responses limited to 90 seconds. Although you may not be asked every question, you should be prepared to respond to all of them.

1. Tell me about yourself.
2. Walk me through your CV.
3. Tell me about your current or most recent role.
4. Why did you leave your last job?
5. Have you ever been asked to leave a position?
6. What do you know about the company?
7. What are your salary requirements? (Never bring up salary first!)
8. Why do you want to work for our company?
9. What is your greatest strength?
10. What is your greatest weakness? (Be positive and position this as an opportunity for improvement.)
11. Why are you interested in this position?
12. Why are you interested in a career change?
13. Are you willing to work evenings and weekends?
14. Are you willing to relocate?
15. Do you have any questions for me?*

*Always have a number of questions prepared. See later in this chapter for suggested questions.

Questions to Ask During the Phone Screen

During most phone screens, you will have an opportunity to ask questions during the final few minutes of the call. Although the primary purpose of the phone screen is for the interviewer to evaluate your potential fit with the role, there are a number of questions you should try to ask if they have not already been discussed, including:

1. Why is the position open? Is this a newly created opening, or did someone leave?
2. What territory does this position cover?
3. What are you looking for in the ideal candidate?
4. Does the role support only one product, therapeutic area, or drug?
5. Who will the role report to?
6. How big is the MSL team?
7. What are the travel expectations?
8. What is the timeline of the hiring process?
9. What is the next step?
10. May I have your email address in case I have any follow-up questions? (Ask this only if you don't have it already.)

Before Ending the Call

✓ Always thank them for their time.
✓ Always mention your excitement for the role and interest in moving forward in the interview process.

The Importance of the Thank-You Email

The thank-you email is an important part of the interview process that is often overlooked by aspiring MSLs but is frequently utilized by experienced MSLs.

In fact, a study conducted by the MSL Society found that 87 percent of U.S.-based MSLs and 66 percent of MSLs globally "always" or "often" write a thank-you Letter after speaking to someone during the MSL interview process (Tables 57 and 58).

Table 57
Survey question: "How often do you write a thank-you letter after speaking to someone during the MSL interview process?"

Writing "Thank You" Letters	
Always	74%
Often	13%
Sometimes	8%
Rarely	2%
Never	1%
I don't recall	2%

2018 "MSL Hiring Practices Survey," MSL Society
303 MSLs (or equivalent title)
U.S. Results

Table 58
Survey question: "How often do you write a thank-you letter after speaking to someone during the MSL interview process?"

Writing "Thank You" Letters	
Always	52%
Often	14%
Sometimes	10%
Rarely	7%
Never	14%
I don't recall	2%

2018 "MSL Hiring Practices Survey," MSL Society
545 MSLs (or equivalent title)
Global Results

Regardless if you think you will be moving forward in the interview process or not, you should send a personalized thank-you email—within twenty-four hours—to every individual you have spoken to or communicated with (recruiters, HR personnel, administrative assistants, etc.) throughout the interview process.

Your thank-you email should further demonstrate your interest in the role, thank the individual for their time, and emphasize how your experience matches the specific requirements of the role. In addition, your thank-you email is an opportunity to highlight key points that were discussed, as well as to share relevant information you did not get to discuss during the call.

Although sending a thank-you email will not guarantee you will be offered the role, it can be an effective way to further demonstrate professionalism and provide a positive impression when several potential candidates have been identified.

The following are formatting guidelines when sending a thank-you email:

✓ Send it within twenty-four hours of the interview.
✓ Write "Thank You" in the subject line.
✓ To increase the chance it will be read, always include your thank-you message directly in the body of the email and not as an attachment.
✓ Use a professional font style, such as Arial or Verdana.
✓ Use a 12-point font for ease of reading.
✓ Use standard black text color.
✓ Proofread it for spelling and grammatical errors before sending.
✓ Limit the text to two or three short paragraphs of three sentences each.

Thank-You Email Template and Content

The thank-you email can be another opportunity to further highlight how your background and experience are a match for the MSL role for which you are applying. However, it's important to keep it brief and relevant. Here are several recommendations:

First Paragraph
- Thank them for taking the time to speak with you.
- Highlight key points and details you discussed during the interview to personalize the message.

Second Paragraph
- Keep it simple and avoid restating your CV.
- Highlight how your background, related accomplishments, and specific experiences fit the needs of the role and will enable you to be successful.

Last Paragraph
- Reiterate your interest and excitement about the role.
- Thank them again for their time and mention you are looking forward to the next step of the hiring process.

The Next Step

If you are successful during the phone screen, you will be contacted after the call to schedule a phone interview with the hiring manager, which is the next step in the process.

The Phone Interview

The phone interview will take place with the hiring manager and is generally arranged by the person with whom you spoke during the phone screen. The purpose of the phone interview is for the hiring manager to evaluate your scientific background, discuss the role, and assess your potential fit. Your success during the phone interview will determine if you will be invited for an in-person interview.

A hiring manager will identify a number of potential candidates and will use the phone interview as a cost-efficient, time-saving method to further narrow down applicants. However, you should use the phone interview as an opportunity to learn more about the role and to make a positive impression on the hiring manager.

During the phone interview, the hiring manager will:

✓ Determine if you have the appropriate therapeutic area and/or disease state experience and scientific knowledge to be successful.

✓ Assess your fit with the MSL team and the hiring manager's management style.

✓ Discuss the needs and responsibilities of the role.

✓ Evaluate your communication skills.

✓ Clarify and discuss details on your CV.

✓ Evaluate your enthusiasm for and interest in the role.

✓ Determine what contributions you can make to the team and the role.

✓ Discuss the territory for the role and travel expectations.

✓ Discuss the next steps in the hiring process (which is typically the in-person interview).

What to Expect During the Phone Interview

Although the format of the phone screen and the phone interview are similar, there are a few important differences. For example, the phone interview will be longer in duration and is typically scheduled for thirty to forty-five minutes. Although the actual duration of the phone interview may vary, the majority last up to forty-five minutes (Tables 59 and 60).

Table 59
Survey question: "On average, how long do you typically speak to an applicant during a phone interview?"

Typical Phone Interview Length	
0 - 15 Minutes	1%
16 - 30 Minutes	39%
31 - 45 Minutes	43%
46 - 60 Minutes	15%
60+ Minutes	1%

2018 "MSL Hiring Practices Survey," MSL Society
97 MSL Managers
U.S. Results

Table 60
Survey question: "On average, how long do you typically speak to an applicant during a phone interview?"

Typical Phone Interview Length	
0 - 15 Minutes	4%
16 - 30 Minutes	40%
31 - 45 Minutes	38%
46 - 60 Minutes	16%
60+ Minutes	2%

2018 "MSL Hiring Practices Survey," MSL Society
185 MSL Managers
Global Results

You should also be prepared to participate in the phone interview virtually using Zoom, Skype, Webex, Microsoft Teams, or other similar software because MSL managers are increasingly utilizing this type of technology as an alternative to the traditional phone interview. Further details are provided in Appendix B regarding how to successfully prepare for virtual interviews.

Regardless of the technology (phone or virtual) utilized, there will be a greater emphasis on your scientific knowledge and background during the phone interview, as well as your ability to demonstrate knowledge of the company products and the therapeutic area and/or disease state the role supports.

The phone interview often begins with the hiring manager providing some background information about themselves and specifics of the role, including how it fits within the structure of the company. Then, the hiring manager will typically ask you to highlight your CV. When highlighting your CV, it's crucial to emphasize how your scientific background, experiences, and accomplishments are relevant to the role. In addition, the hiring manager will evaluate your communication skills by focusing on how you present information and how you respond to questions.

The final ten or fifteen minutes of the interview are usually set aside to provide you with an opportunity to ask questions. Your questions should be based on your research of the company and the role, their products, topics that arose during the interview, and other topics that may not have been discussed but are relevant.

Although the phone interview will take place with the hiring manager, it is a common practice for a hiring manager to ask an MSL on their team to also interview applicants. A study conducted by the MSL Society found that 74 percent of U.S.-based MSL managers and 54 percent of global MSL managers "always" or "often" have MSLs from their team interview applicants (Tables 61 and 62).

Table 61

Survey question: "Typically, how often is an applicant interviewed by MSLs on your team during the phone or in-person interviews?"

Interviewed by MSLs on Team	
Always	49%
Often	25%
Sometimes	13%
Rarely	9%
Never	3%

2018 "MSL Hiring Practices Survey," MSL Society
97 MSL Managers
U.S. Results

Table 62

Survey question: "Typically, how often is an applicant interviewed by MSLs on your team during the phone or in-person interviews?"

Interviewed by MSLs on Team	
Always	31%
Often	23%
Sometimes	16%
Rarely	14%
Never	16%

2018 "MSL Hiring Practices Survey," MSL Society
185 MSL Managers
Global Results

Strategies for a Successful Phone Interview

Many of the strategies for success are the same for the phone screen and the phone interview. As with the phone screen, your preparation and communication skills during the phone interview will determine your success.

The phone interview will likely be your first opportunity to verbally express to the hiring manager how your background and experience match the needs of the role for which they are hiring. As a result, it's essential to be fully prepared.

The following are a number of recommendations to help you prepare for the phone interview:

Before the Call

✓ Review and follow all relevant techniques and suggestions from the phone screen section.

✓ Research the hiring manager using LinkedIn and other techniques described in Chapter 3.

✓ Have a printed copy of your CV in front of you. The exception to this is if the interview is being conducted virtually on camera utilizing Zoom, Skype, Webex, Microsoft Teams, or other similar technology where the hiring manager will be able to see you. During a virtual interview, having printed material in front of you can be distracting and make you appear unprepared.

✓ Be prepared to discuss every detail of your CV. The hiring manager will use your CV as a basis for their questions.

✓ Research the company, including reviewing their website, to ensure you are thoroughly familiar with the product(s) the MSL team supports.

✓ Be prepared to have a detailed discussion regarding the science of the product(s) the MSL role supports.

✓ Be prepared to have a detailed scientific discussion regarding your background and how it matches the needs of the role.

✓ Practice succinct answers to the traditional type questions that may be asked (see later in the chapter for specific questions) to convey confidence and demonstrate scientific knowledge.

✓ Review the "Behavioral Type Questions" section later in this chapter to successfully prepare for this type of question.

✓ Be prepared with a response if asked about a perceived weakness. Provide examples of how you have addressed the weakness and have already improved.

✓ Be able to address your lack of MSL experience with succinct examples of accomplishments and skills relevant to the role, as well as the value you bring to the team.

✓ Review notes taken during the phone screen to help you prepare a list of questions for the hiring manager.

✓ Plan to take notes during the phone interview for reference when preparing for the in-person interview. However, if the interview will be conducted virtually on camera and the hiring manager will be able to see you, inform the manager you will be taking notes on important points being discussed.

✓ Prepare a number of questions to ask the hiring manager. See later in the chapter for suggested questions.

✓ Be prepared to speak at least fifteen minutes before the call is scheduled to begin.

One of the most important elements of successful preparation is thoroughly researching every individual with whom you will be interviewing with throughout all stages of the MSL interview process. In fact, a survey revealed that 88 percent of MSLs in the U.S. and 85 percent of MSLs globally "always" or "often" research the individuals with whom they will be interviewing with for an MSL role (Tables 63 and 64).

Table 63
Survey question: "When preparing for an interview: How often do you research the individuals that you will be interviewing with for an MSL role utilizing sources such as LinkedIn, MSL Society member directory, social media, etc.?"

Researching Interviewers	
Always	73%
Often	15%
Sometimes	8%
Rarely	2%
Never	2%

2018 "MSL Hiring Practices Survey," MSL Society
303 MSLs (or equivalent title)
U.S. Results

Table 64
Survey question: "When preparing for an interview: How often do you research the individuals that you will be interviewing with for an MSL role utilizing sources such as LinkedIn, MSL Society member directory, social media, etc.?"

Researching Interviewers	
Always	67%
Often	18%
Sometimes	8%
Rarely	4%
Never	3%

2018 "MSL Hiring Practices Survey," MSL Society
545 MSLs (or equivalent title)
Global Results

During the Call

✓ Apply all applicable techniques and suggestions from the phone screen section.

✓ Always remain positive and be fully engaged throughout the call.

✓ Take notes to capture key points; however, note-taking should not distract you from engaging in the conversation or actively listening. In addition, if the interview is being conducted virtually on camera, and you are visible to the hiring manager, inform them you will be taking notes on important points being discussed.

✓ Pay attention to the volume and pace of your voice to ensure it's appropriate.

✓ Demonstrate your knowledge of the role, the company, and the science of the product(s) the MSL team supports.

✓ Emphasize how your scientific background, knowledge, skills, and accomplishments are a match to the needs of the role and will have an immediate, positive impact on the MSL team.

✓ Be sure to mention any relevant experiences that are not on your CV or any that have not been discussed.

✓ Never mislead or misrepresent anything regarding your background or experience.

✓ When responding to questions, answer only the question asked; do not deviate into unrelated topics.

✓ Avoid rambling when responding to questions by limiting your answers to 90 seconds and pausing to allow the hiring manager to interject comments or questions.

✓ Occasionally confirm you have completely answered a question with a response such as, "Did I answer your question?"

✓ Don't ever ask to skip a question. If you encounter an unexpected question, asking the manager to rephrase the question can provide you additional time to formulate an appropriate response.

✓ Interject relevant questions, as appropriate, throughout the call to learn more about the hiring manager and to gain a better understanding of the role, as well as the company.

✓ Never initiate a discussion regarding salary or benefits with the hiring manager. Refer to Chapter 8 for guidelines on how to address questions related to salary and benefits expectations.

In addition, throughout the conversation, it's important to express enthusiasm for the role, the company, and the science of the company's products. In fact, according to a survey, 91 percent of U.S.-based MSL managers and 84 percent of MSL managers globally revealed that it is "very important" for an applicant to demonstrate enthusiasm during a phone or in-person interview (Tables 65 and 66).

Table 65
Survey question: "How important is it for an applicant to demonstrate enthusiasm during a phone or in-person interview?"

Demonstrating Enthusiasm	
Very Important	91%
Somewhat Important	9%
Neutral	0%
Not Very Important	0%
Not At All Important	0%

2018 "MSL Hiring Practices Survey," MSL Society
97 MSL Managers
U.S. Results

Table 66
Survey question: "How important is it for an applicant to demonstrate enthusiasm during a phone or in-person interview?"

Demonstrating Enthusiasm	
Very Important	84%
Somewhat Important	14%
Neutral	1%
Not Very Important	0%
Not At All Important	1%

2018 "MSL Hiring Practices Survey," MSL Society
185 MSL Managers
Global Results

Questions You May Be Asked During a Phone Interview

A hiring manager may ask you a variety of questions during a phone interview, some of which will be similar to those of the phone screen. However, during the phone interview, the manager will expect your answers to be much more specific and detailed regarding how your scientific background and experiences are relevant to the role. Ultimately, you need to convince the manager that you possess the requisite scientific knowledge and experience to be successful in the role.

The hiring manager may ask traditional or behavioral type questions or a combination of both during an interview. However, you typically will not know prior to the interview which type of questions will be asked. As a result, it's important to know the difference between the two types of questions and be prepared to answer both.

Traditional Type Questions

Traditional questions are broad in scope and generally focus on an applicant's perceptions, observations, and goals. The MSL manager will expect direct, succinct responses.

Traditional questions are generally less stressful than behavioral questions. Although you may not be asked every question, you should be prepared to respond to all the following traditional questions:

1. Walk me through your CV.
2. Tell me about your experience with the therapeutic area and/or disease state or the science of the product the MSL supports.

3. Do you have any experience working with KOLs in this specific therapeutic area?
4. Tell me about your current or most recent role.
5. Why are you interested in this specific role?
6. What do you know about the company?
7. How does this role fit with your long-term career goals?
8. Why are you interested in a career change?
9. What is your most significant professional accomplishment to date?
10. Are you willing to work evenings and weekends?
11. Why do you want to work for this company?
12. Why are you a good fit for this role?
13. Are you willing to relocate?
14. Are you a team player?
15. Do you have any questions for me?*

*Always have a number of questions prepared. See later in this chapter for suggested questions.

Behavioral Type Questions

Behavioral questions are more specific and focus on your experience in work-related scenarios.

This type of interview question is based on the concept that past behavior is a predictor of future performance, and by utilizing it, an interviewer will be able to better predict how you might perform in an MSL role. Common behavioral questions typically begin with phrases such as, "Describe a time when..." or "Provide an example of..."

An MSL manager will have determined what skills are needed for the role and will ask questions to determine if you have those skills. When asked a behavioral question, you will be expected to provide details that highlight your experience related to that situation. It's important to provide specific examples that demonstrate evidence of your past performance in relevant situations.

An effective technique for answering behavioral questions is to utilize the STAR method, which includes four components:

- Situation: Identify a specific situation that had a positive outcome.
- Task: Describe the tasks involved in the situation.
- Action: Specify the actions you took to achieve results.
- Results: Describe what happened due to your actions.

Using this method will ensure that you include specific results in your responses without rambling.

However, answering behavioral questions can be stressful if you are not prepared. Although it is impossible to know the exact questions you may be asked, you should have a number of relevant examples prepared that are applicable to the MSL role so that you are successful in answering this type of question.

Behavioral interview questions provide you the opportunity to demonstrate your talent, ability, and results. When preparing, consider the type of competencies most important to the MSL profession (e.g., scientific aptitude, communication skills, being a team player, building relationships, etc.) and practice responses incorporating compelling anecdotes and specific examples based on your experience utilizing all four components of the STAR method.

When practicing, rehearse responses aloud and record them. This will enable you to review and better prepare for this type of question.

Behavioral questions are commonly utilized by MSL managers. In fact, an MSL Society survey found that 71 percent of MSL managers globally and 69 percent of U.S.-based MSL mangers "always" or "often" utilize behavioral questions (Tables 67 and 68).

Table 67
Survey question: "During the phone or in-person interview, do you utilize behavioral questions (i.e., 'Tell me a time when you...')?"

Use of Behavioral Type Questions	
Always	40%
Often	31%
Sometimes	22%
Rarely	6%
Never	1%

2018 "MSL Hiring Practices Survey," MSL Society
185 MSL Managers
Global Results

Table 68
Survey question: "During the phone or in-person interview, do you utilize behavioral questions (i.e., 'Tell me a time when you...')?"

Use of Behavioral Type Questions	
Always	40%
Often	29%
Sometimes	22%
Rarely	9%
Never	0%

2018 "MSL Hiring Practices Survey," MSL Society
97 MSL Managers
U.S. Results

Questions to Ask During the Phone Interview

As mentioned, the purpose of the phone interview is for the hiring manager to evaluate your scientific background and potential fit with the role by asking you a number of questions. However, there are several questions you should ask as well (if they have not already been discussed) to gain a better understanding of the role, including:

1. Why is this position open?
2. Is this a newly created role or did someone leave?

3. What is the geographical territory for the role?
4. What are the travel expectations?
5. What are you looking for in the ideal candidate?
6. What are the critical factors for success in the job?
7. How many products, therapeutic areas, or drugs does the role support?
8. Are there existing relationships with KOLs in the territory?
9. How big is the MSL team?
10. What is the hiring process?
11. What is the next step in the process?
12. What is a realistic timeline for hiring?
13. Have I answered all your questions?
14. After our discussion today, how do you think I would potentially fit within the role, the team, and the company?
15. May I have your email address in case I have any follow-up questions? (Ask this only if you don't have it already.)

Before Ending the Call

✓ Always thank the manager for their time.
✓ Always mention your excitement for the role and interest in moving forward in the interview process.

Most Common Reasons MSL Managers Reject Applicants During a Phone Interview

As an aspiring MSL, it's important to be aware of the most common reasons that MSL managers do not move an applicant forward in the hiring process. A survey conducted by the MSL Society revealed that "poor phone or communication skills," "unpolished communication," "lack of enthusiasm," and "being unprepared" were four of the most common reasons MSL managers globally and U.S.-based MSL managers reject an applicant during a phone interview (Tables 69 and 70). Be sure to avoid these critical mistakes.

Table 69
Survey question: "Typically, during a phone interview, what are the most common reasons that prevent you from moving an applicant forward in the hiring process (i.e., in-person interview)? (Check all that apply.)"

Reason for Not Moving Forward – Phone Interview			
Poor phone or communication skills	63%	Provides inaccurate or false details about their academic background, experience, or other details	36%
Unpolished communication	63%	Inability to match background/experiences to the needs of the role	34%
Lack of enthusiasm	62%	Inconsistent answers	31%
Lack of understanding of the MSL role	58%	Concern regarding frequent job changes	31%
Being unprepared	57%	Does not articulate relevant therapeutic area and/or disease state experience	28%
Being arrogant	54%	Not asking relevant questions	28%
Lack of knowledge of the company or our product(s)	49%	Dominating the conversation	23%
Being awkward or weird - inability to carry on a "normal" conversation	48%	Appearing desperate	23%
Poor cultural fit	43%	Inability to address concern regarding lack of or limited MSL experience	22%
Lack of connection with applicant	42%	Speaking negatively about the role of sales representatives	21%
Failing to be succinct when answering questions	40%	Applicant inquiries about salary or benefits	17%
Being unprofessional	40%	Not knowing all the details on their CV/Resume	16%
Speaking negatively about current or previous employer, manager, team	40%	Concern regarding career gaps	9%
Failing to fully answer questions asked	38%	Lack of "Thank-You" email and follow up to express continued interest	9%
Inability to address "why this job?"	37%	Other (please specify)	2%

2018 "MSL Hiring Practices Survey," MSL Society
97 MSL Managers
U.S. Results

Table 70
Survey question: "Typically, during a phone interview, what are the most common reasons that prevent you from moving an applicant forward in the hiring process (i.e., in-person interview)? (Check all that apply.)"

Reason for Not Moving Forward – Phone Interview			
Poor phone or communication skills	63%	Inability to match background/experiences to the needs of the role	33%
Lack of enthusiasm	57%	Failing to fully answer questions asked	33%
Being unprepared	56%	Failing to be succinct when answering questions	33%
Unpolished communication	56%	Speaking negatively about the role of sales representatives	27%
Being arrogant	54%	Concern regarding frequent job changes	25%
Lack of understanding of the MSL role	53%	Not asking relevant questions	24%
Being awkward or weird - inability to carry on a "normal" conversation	48%	Does not articulate relevant therapeutic area and/or disease state experience	22%
Being unprofessional	47%	Not knowing all the details on their CV/Resume	22%
Inconsistent answers	43%	Inability to address concern regarding lack of or limited MSL experience	22%
Provides inaccurate or false details about their academic background, experience, or other details	42%	Dominating the conversation	20%
Speaking negatively about current or previous employer, manager, team	41%	Appearing desperate	19%
Lack of knowledge of the company or our product(s)	39%	Applicant inquiries about salary or benefits	13%
Lack of connection with applicant	38%	Concern regarding career gaps	10%
Poor cultural fit	36%	Lack of "Thank-You" email and follow up to express continued interest	8%
Inability to address "why this job?"	36%	Other (please specify)	3%

2018 "MSL Hiring Practices Survey," MSL Society
185 MSL Managers
Global Results

The Importance of the Thank-You Email

As stated previously in the phone screen section, sending a thank-you email is important. In fact, the majority of MSLs in the U.S. and globally "always" or "often" send them. The results of a survey highlight the importance of sending a thank-you email according to MSL managers as well. The survey revealed 71 percent of U.S.-based MSL managers and 51 percent of MSL managers globally indicated receiving a thank-you letter or email from an applicant is "very important" or "somewhat important" after a phone or an in-person interview (Tables 71 and 72).

Table 71
Survey question: "How important is receiving a thank-you letter or email from an applicant after a phone or an in-person interview?"

Value of "Thank You" Letter	
Very Important	26%
Somewhat Important	45%
Neutral	24%
Not Very Important	2%
Not At All Important	3%

2018 "MSL Hiring Practices Survey," MSL Society
97 MSL Managers
U.S. Results

Table 72
Survey question: "How important is receiving a thank-you letter or email from an applicant after a phone or an in-person interview?"

Value of "Thank You" Letter	
Very Important	19%
Somewhat Important	32%
Neutral	29%
Not Very Important	11%
Not At All Important	9%

2018 "MSL Hiring Practices Survey," MSL Society
185 MSL Managers
Global Results

If necessary, review the phone screen section for detailed recommended guidelines for sending a thank-you email. Although the guidelines for the phone interview are similar to those for the phone screen, when sending a thank-you email to the hiring manager, be sure to emphasize how your scientific background matches the needs of the role.

The Next Step

If you are successful during the phone interview, you will be notified after the call to schedule an in-person interview, which is typically the next step in the hiring process.

7

The In-Person Interview

It's important to be aware that the hiring manager will only select a few candidates to invite for in-person interviews.

In fact, according to the results of an MSL Society survey, 97 percent of U.S.-based MSL managers and 90 percent of MSL managers globally interview a maximum of five applicants in person before making a hiring decision (Tables 73 and 74). Therefore, if you make it to this step in the hiring process, you will be competing with a small group of other candidates. As a result, it's crucial you thoroughly prepare.

Table 73

Survey question: "Typically, how many MSL applicants are interviewed during the in-person interview before making a hiring decision?"

Number of Applicants Interviewed	
1	0%
2	16%
3	53%
4	18%
5	10%
6	2%
7	1%
8	0%
8+ (please specify)	0%

2018 "MSL Hiring Practices Survey," MSL Society
97 MSL Managers
U.S. Results

Table 74

Survey question: "Typically, how many MSL applicants are interviewed during the in-person interview before making a hiring decision?"

Number of Applicants Interviewed	
1	1%
2	14%
3	45%
4	16%
5	14%
6	6%
7	2%
8	2%
8+ (please specify)	1%

2018 "MSL Hiring Practices Survey," MSL Society
185 MSL Managers
Global Results

The in-person interview will typically be conducted at the company headquarters or at a regional office. The in-person interview may also be conducted virtually. Rarely, a second round of in-person interviews or panel interviews may be requested.

After the date is set for the in-person interview, you will be provided a complete itinerary, including the names and titles of those with whom you will be meeting, as well as the full schedule for the day and what is required. However, be aware the itinerary may change throughout the day, including the individuals you are scheduled to meet.

In addition, if you need to travel, the company will either arrange your flight and hotel reservation or provide guidelines on how to make your own travel arrangements. In either scenario, in most countries, the company will pay for all interview-related expenses, including all travel expenses, meals, and any incidentals. If you need to travel, always arrive the day before the interview to give yourself sufficient time to get settled and prepared. Traveling the day before will also enable you to avoid any unexpected travel glitches you might encounter if you were to travel on the day of the interview.

During the in-person interviews, you will meet the hiring manager, along with other key decision-makers from other departments. The purpose of the in-person interview is for the hiring manager and other key decision-makers to evaluate your scientific background, discuss the role, assess your potential fit, and ultimately determine if you will be offered the role. You should approach the in-person interview as an opportunity to learn more about the role, the company, and the decision makers with whom you will be meeting throughout the day. Using the strategies described in previous chapters, you should research each person with whom you are scheduled to meet and become familiar with their professional backgrounds. Doing this research may also provide information you can use to make a personal connection with the interviewer. Your goal is to make a positive impression on everyone with whom you meet or engage during each interview.

Throughout the day, each interviewer will:

✓ Discuss their role, department, and how they interact with the MSL team.

✓ Evaluate your therapeutic area experience and scientific knowledge.

✓ Clarify and discuss details on your CV.

✓ Assess your ability to work effectively with their team or department.

✓ Discuss the needs and responsibilities of the role.

✓ Evaluate your communication and possibly your presentation skills.

✓ Assess your personality fit with the company.

✓ Determine what contributions you can make to the company.

✓ Evaluate your enthusiasm for and interest in the role.

✓ Clarify your understanding of the responsibilities of the role.

What to Expect During the In-Person Interview

During the in-person interview, you will likely meet with multiple decision makers, including the hiring manager and other key decision makers who typically work with the MSL team at the company. In addition to meeting with each of them individually, you may also be required, at some point during the day, to deliver a scientific PowerPoint presentation.

Depending on the company, the key decision makers you meet with may include staff from the following departments:

• Marketing (e.g., marketing manager or a director of marketing)

• Regulatory affairs (e.g., director of regulatory affairs)

- Sales (e.g., national sales director)
- Medical affairs (e.g., senior MSL or a director of medical information)
- Human resources

Typically, each interview will last thirty to sixty minutes and will take place in a conference room or in each individual's office. The interviews will likely begin with each individual providing some background information about themselves and how their role or department interacts with the MSL team. The interviewer will likely ask you a number of questions about your background, your knowledge of the company's product(s), and possibly the therapeutic area or disease state the MSL role supports. When addressing these questions, it's important to convince the interviewer that your background, experiences, and accomplishments match the needs of the role. Throughout each interview, you will also have an opportunity to ask questions. Your questions should be based on your research of the company, its products, the role, and other topics that may not have been discussed but are relevant to the position.

Although the MSL manager will make the final hiring decision, they will rely on the opinions of the other key decision makers with whom you meet throughout the day to determine if you will be offered the position. In fact, a survey conducted by the MSL Society found that both globally and in the U.S., the hiring manager alone decides if an applicant will be offered a position the majority of the time (Tables 75 and 76).

Table 75
Survey question: "Ultimately, who decides if an applicant will be offered a position?"

Final Hiring Decision-Maker	
Me (as the manager)	64%
Combination of all three	31%
Other (please specify)	4%
HR	0%
My direct manager	0%

2018 "MSL Hiring Practices Survey," MSL Society
96 MSL Managers
U.S. Results

Table 76
Survey question: "Ultimately, who decides if an applicant will be offered a position?"

Final Hiring Decision-Maker	
Me (as the manager)	54%
Combination of all three	41%
Other (please specify)	3%
HR	1%
My direct manager	1%

2018 "MSL Hiring Practices Survey," MSL Society
185 MSL Managers
Global Results

Strategies for a Successful In-Person Interview

Many of the strategies for success are the same for the phone screen, phone interview, and in-person interviews. The following sections include recommendations for the PowerPoint presentation, what to wear, and how to prepare for the interview.

PowerPoint Presentation

As mentioned in the previous chapter, your preparation and communication skills will determine your success throughout the hiring process. One of the most important communication skills necessary to be successful in the MSL role is the ability to effectively present scientific information.

In fact, a survey conducted by the MSL Society revealed that 78 percent of U.S.-based MSL managers and 77 percent of MSL managers globally reported it is "very important" for an applicant to demonstrate strong presentation skills when making a hiring decision (Tables 77 and 78).

Table 77
Survey question: "How important is it for an applicant to demonstrate strong presentation skills when making a hiring decision?"

Importance of Presentation Skills	
Very Important	78%
Somewhat Important	21%
Neutral	1%
Not Very Important	0%
Not At All Important	0%

2018 "MSL Hiring Practices Survey," MSL Society
87 MSL Managers
U.S. Results

Table 78
Survey question: "How important is it for an applicant to demonstrate strong presentation skills when making a hiring decision?"

Importance of Presentation Skills	
Very Important	77%
Somewhat Important	20%
Neutral	3%
Not Very Important	0%
Not At All Important	0%

2018 "MSL Hiring Practices Survey," MSL Society
159 MSL Managers
Global Results

As a result, delivering a scientific PowerPoint presentation to demonstrate this ability is commonly required during the in-person interview.

This same survey revealed that 90 percent of U.S.-based MSL managers and 86 percent of MSL managers globally require applicants to deliver a presentation during the interview process (Tables 79 and 80).

Table 79
Survey question: "Typically, are applicants required to deliver a presentation during the interview process?"

Presentation Requirement	
Yes	90%
No	10%

2018 "MSL Hiring Practices Survey," MSL Society
97 MSL Managers
U.S. Results

Table 80
Survey question: "Typically, are applicants required to deliver a presentation during the interview process?"

Presentation Requirement	
Yes	86%
No	14%

2018 "MSL Hiring Practices Survey," MSL Society
185 MSL Managers
Global Results

You will receive details and guidelines for the presentation prior to the interview, including any request to cover specific content (e.g., product or disease state), the expected format, and the length. Although the expected length of the presentation will vary, according to a survey conducted by MSL Society, 90 percent of MSL interview presentations in the U.S. and 93 percent globally are thirty minutes or less (Tables 81 and 82).

Table 81
Survey question: "Typically, how long is the presentation?"

Typical Presentation Length	
1-10 minutes	2%
11-20 minutes	40%
21-30 minutes	48%
31-45 minutes	9%
45+ minutes	0%

2018 "MSL Hiring Practices Survey," MSL Society
87 MSL Managers
U.S. Results

Table 82
Survey question: "Typically, how long is the presentation?"

Typical Presentation Length	
1-10 minutes	15%
11-20 minutes	42%
21-30 minutes	36%
31-45 minutes	6%
45+ minutes	1%

2018 "MSL Hiring Practices Survey," MSL Society
159 MSL Managers
Global Results

Generally, the audience for the presentation will consist of those with whom you are scheduled to meet throughout the day. During the presentation, each of them will evaluate both your presentation skills and how you engage with the audience.

One frequent question asked by aspiring MSLs is whether they will be allowed to choose any topic for their PowerPoint presentation. Depending on where you are located, the answer will differ. A survey revealed that while the majority of U.S.-based MSL managers allow applicants to choose any topic to present during the interview, the majority of MSL managers globally do not (Tables 83 and 84).

Table 83
Survey question: "Are applicants allowed to choose any topic they want to present?"

Applicants Given Topic Choice	
Yes	63%
No	37%

2018 "MSL Hiring Practices Survey," MSL Society
87 MSL Managers
U.S. Results

Table 84
Survey question: "Are applicants allowed to choose any topic they want to present?"

Applicants Given Topic Choice	
Yes	44%
No	56%

2018 "MSL Hiring Practices Survey," MSL Society
159 MSL Managers
Global Results

If you are allowed to choose any disease state, product, or drug as the topic for the presentation, you should avoid presenting on any of the company's products. Selecting one of the company's products as the topic for the presentation is one of the most common mistakes candidates make. Although intuitively this might seem like a great idea that would enable you to demonstrate your understanding of the company's products, you should instead select a disease state or drug in which you already have extensive experience or knowledge. You want to be the expert in the room!

Your goal is to deliver a polished presentation that enables you to position yourself as a subject-matter expert and demonstrate your presentation skills. This will not be possible if you choose to present on one of the company's products for which you have little knowledge or experience. Furthermore, those in the audience will already be subject-matter experts on their products, so in the event you make a mistake during the presentation, it will be immediately obvious to everyone there. This mistake is easily avoided by presenting on a drug or disease state for which you (not the those in the audience) have extensive experience or knowledge.

The following are a number of additional suggestions for a successful presentation:

- Use a professional template with a light-colored background and a contrasting color for the text.

- Limit the number of slides to a maximum of fifteen for a twenty-minute presentation.
- Avoid using animation, sounds, etc. because the presentation should demonstrate your ability to present, not highlight PowerPoint features.
- Proofread your presentation to avoid spelling, grammatical, and punctuation errors.
- Save your presentation to a flash drive and email a copy to yourself as a backup.
- Rehearse the presentation multiple times before the interview.
- Know every detail on each slide, including all statistics.
- Never read directly from the slides, and limit the amount of information on each slide.
- Never use a laser pointer because few people are good at using them and they are often distracting to the audience.
- Don't overwhelm the audience with technical details or too much information.
- Throughout the presentation, use keywords from the job description or company website.

What to Wear

During an in-person interview, the first impression you make is crucially important. Your appearance is critical in making a positive first impression and will also contribute to your success during the interview. Everyone with whom you meet throughout the day will evaluate how you present yourself, as well as how you might present yourself to KOLs or other health care providers. Part of each interviewer's evaluation will be based on your appearance and attire.

Regardless if you will be interviewing with a pharmaceutical, biotechnology, medical device, or another company type, applicants are expected to wear business attire. This will further help make a positive first impression. Although the definition of "business attire" may differ depending on where you are geographically located, the following are suggestions and guidelines that are generally applicable for what to wear during an in-person MSL interview:

Men

- ✓ A solid, dark-color (blue, dark gray, black) suit
- ✓ A white, long-sleeve shirt (avoid button-down collars)
- ✓ A silk tie
- ✓ Polished lace-up dress shoes
- ✓ Clean-shaven or well-groomed facial hair
- ✓ Well-groomed hair
- ✓ Clean, trimmed nails
- ✓ No cologne
- ✓ A portfolio (to carry copies of your CV and for note-taking)

Women

- ✓ A solid, dark-color (blue, dark gray, black) conservative dress, skirt, or pant suit
- ✓ A conservative top or blouse (if wearing a skirt or pant suit)
- ✓ Polished closed-toe shoes
- ✓ A professional hairstyle
- ✓ Light makeup
- ✓ Limited jewelry
- ✓ Manicured nails
- ✓ No perfume
- ✓ A portfolio (to carry copies of your CV and for note-taking)

Professional Body Language

In addition to your appearance, projecting professional body language is also critical in making a positive impression on everyone you meet and will contribute to your success during each interview. See the "Make a positive impression" section in Chapter 4 for additional techniques regarding making a positive impression. Part of making a positive impression will be based on the manner in which you greet and engage with each interviewer. Utilize the following techniques to project professional body language throughout each interview:

- Greet each interviewer enthusiastically as you introduce yourself, smile, and thank them for taking the time to speak with you.
- Shake hands, when appropriate. See the "Properly shake hands" section in Chapter 4 for specific recommendations on how to shake hands professionally.
- Maintain an appropriate distance from others (don't stand or sit too closely).
- Directly face the person with whom you are speaking.
- Always sit up straight in your chair with your shoulders square to the interviewer.
- When standing, maintain an upright posture with your head up, shoulders back, and square to the individual with whom you are speaking.
- While sitting, your feet should be flat on the floor with your arms unfolded at your sides or resting on a table or desk.
- Create a connection by consistently making eye contact throughout the interview.
- Smile occasionally, when appropriate.
- Throughout each interview, speak clearly, and be aware of the volume of your voice (avoid speaking too loudly or too softly).
- While listening, acknowledge the interviewer by nodding to communicate you are engaged.
- Use hand gestures when appropriate, but keep your movements close to your body (avoid excessive gesturing).

- Do not fidget with your hands.
- Don't sway, rock, or pace when speaking.
- Don't keep your hands in your pockets.
- Avoid touching your face.

Preparation

The famous expression, "Those who fail to prepare are absolutely preparing to fail," is certainly applicable to an MSL in-person interview. It is essential to prepare for success. The following are several strategies that will help you prepare.

Before the Interview

✓ Review and follow all relevant techniques and suggestions from the phone screen section.

✓ Research the hiring manager and everyone else with whom you are scheduled to meet by using LinkedIn and other techniques described in Chapter 3.

✓ Print and take with you enough copies of your CV for every person with whom you are scheduled to meet.

✓ Be prepared to discuss every detail of your CV. The hiring manager and others you will meet throughout the interview will use your CV as a basis for their questions.

✓ Research the company, including their website, to ensure you are thoroughly familiar with the products the MSL team supports.

✓ Be prepared to have a detailed discussion regarding the science of the product(s) the MSL role supports.

✓ Be prepared to have a detailed scientific discussion regarding your background and how it matches the needs of the role.

✓ Practice succinct answers to the typical traditional type questions that may be asked (see later in the chapter for specific questions) to convey confidence and demonstrate scientific knowledge.

✓ Review the "Behavioral Type Questions" section in the previous chapter to successfully prepare for this type of question.

✓ Be prepared with a response if asked about a perceived weakness. Provide examples of how you have addressed the weakness and have already improved.

✓ Be able to address your lack of MSL experience with succinct examples of accomplishments and skills relevant to the role, as well as the value you bring to the team.

✓ Utilize the notes you took during the phone interview to prepare for the in-person interview.

✓ Prepare a number of questions to ask the hiring manager and each interviewer (see later in the chapter for suggested questions).

✓ Print the job description and take it with you to review the night before the in-person interview.

✓ Know the exact address and building (if necessary) where the interview is being held.

During the Interview

There are also several strategies that will help you be successful during the in-person interview, including:

✓ Apply all applicable techniques and suggestions from the phone screen and phone interview sections.

✓ Don't ever be late. Arrive at least twenty minutes before the first interview is scheduled to begin.

✓ Know the name of the individual you are supposed to ask for when you arrive at the company.

✓ Greet each person enthusiastically with a firm handshake and a smile when you are introduced.

✓ Always remain positive and be fully engaged with each individual.

✓ Demonstrate your knowledge of the role, the company, and the science of the product(s) the MSL team supports.

✓ With each interviewer, emphasize how your scientific background, knowledge, skills, and accomplishments match the needs of the role and how you will have an immediate positive impact on the MSL team and the company.

✓ Throughout each interview, show enthusiasm for the role, the company, and the science of the company's products.

✓ Sit up straight to clearly project your voice and to convey confidence.

✓ Maintain professional body language throughout each interview.

✓ Project confidence by maintaining eye contact when responding to questions.

✓ Use verbal cues (e.g., "I see" and "I understand") to indicate you are following the conversation.

✓ Enunciate and speak clearly when responding to or asking questions.

✓ Pay attention to the volume and pace of your voice to ensure it's appropriate.

✓ Occasionally confirm you have completely answered a question with a response such as, "Did I answer your question?"

✓ When responding to questions, answer only the question asked; do not deviate into unrelated topics.

- ✓ Be sure to mention any relevant experiences that are not on your CV or any that have not been discussed.
- ✓ Never mislead or misrepresent anything regarding your background or experience.
- ✓ Avoid rambling when responding to questions by limiting your answers to ninety seconds and pausing to allow the interviewer to interject comments or questions.
- ✓ Don't ever ask to skip a question. If you encounter an unexpected question, asking the interviewer to rephrase the question can provide you additional time to formulate an appropriate response.
- ✓ Interject relevant questions, as appropriate, throughout each interview to gain a better understanding of how the MSL role works with their department.
- ✓ Never initiate a discussion regarding salary or benefits. Refer to Chapter 8 for guidelines on how to address questions related to salary and benefits expectations.

One final crucial strategy to implement during each in-person interview is to demonstrate you are coachable, which essentially means you are humble, open to instruction or observation, receptive to new ideas and change, and willing to learn new approaches to challenges. Ensure to incorporate the various characteristics of coachability in your responses to questions from each interviewer to demonstrate this important quality.

Coachability is essential to MSL managers! In fact, according to a survey, 88 percent of U.S.-based MSL managers and 84 percent of MSL managers globally reported that it is "very important" for an MSL to be coachable (Tables 85 and 86).

Table 85
Survey question: "How important is it for an MSL to be 'coachable'?"

Importance of Being Coachable	
Very Important	88%
Somewhat Important	11%
Neutral	1%
Not Very Important	0%
Not At All Important	0%

2018 "MSL Hiring Practices Survey," MSL Society
97 MSL Managers
U.S. Results

Table 86
Survey question: "How important is it for an MSL to be 'coachable'?"

Importance of Being Coachable	
Very Important	84%
Somewhat Important	14%
Neutral	2%
Not Very Important	0%
Not At All Important	0%

2018 "MSL Hiring Practices Survey," MSL Society
185 MSL Managers
Global Results

Questions You May Be Asked During an In-Person Interview

There are a variety of questions an interviewer may ask during the in-person interview. Some of these questions may be the same as those asked during the phone screen or phone interview. However, it is expected that your answers at this stage will include greater detail as to how your scientific background and experiences are a fit with the role. Ultimately, each interviewer will evaluate if you have the necessary skills and background to be successful in the role.

Throughout the in-person interviews, the hiring manager and others will likely ask a combination of both traditional and behavioral type questions. As a result, it's important to know the difference between the two types of questions and be prepared to answer both. Regardless of the type of question you are asked, all your responses should focus on the needs of the role. Whenever possible, this should include highlighting your direct experience with the specific therapeutic area or disease state the role supports.

Traditional Type Questions

Again, traditional questions are broad in scope and generally focus on an applicant's perceptions, observations, and goals. The MSL manager and others will be expecting direct, succinct responses.

Although you may not be asked every question, you should be prepared to respond to all the following traditional questions:

1. Tell me about yourself, or walk me through your CV.
2. Tell me about your education.
3. Tell me about your current or most recent role.
4. Why are you interested in a career change?
5. What do you know about the company?
6. Why do you want to work for this company?
7. Why are you interested in this specific role?
8. Why are you a good fit for this role?
9. How does this role fit with your long-term career goals?
10. Tell me about your experience with the therapeutic area or the science of our company's products.
11. What experience do you have working in a cross-functional manner with marketing, sales, regulatory, etc.?
12. Do you have any experience working with KOLs in this specific therapeutic area?

13. What is your most significant professional accomplishment to date?

14. What are your strengths and weaknesses?

15. Do you have any questions for me?*

*Always have a number of questions prepared. See later in this chapter for suggested questions.

Behavioral Type Questions

As mentioned in the previous chapter, 71 percent of MSL managers globally and 69 percent of U.S.-based MSL mangers "always" or "often" utilize behavioral questions during the phone or in-person interview. In addition, others that you will interview with may also utilize behavioral questions. As a result, it's important to be prepared and able to provide a number of relevant examples—utilizing the STAR format—that are applicable to the MSL role. If necessary, review the behavioral question section in Chapter 6.

Questions to Ask During the In-Person Interview

As with previous stages in the interviewing process, the purpose of the in-person interview is for the hiring manager and other key decision makers to evaluate your scientific background and potential fit with the role by asking you a number of questions. However, there are several questions you should ask as well (if they have not already been discussed) to gain a better understanding of the role, including:

Questions for the Hiring Manager

1. Who makes up the medical affairs team for this therapeutic area? What are their roles?
2. What is the relationship of the medical affairs department and the MSL team with the rest of the company?
3. With whom does the MSL team role work cross functionally?
4. What are the top priorities of the role over the next three months? Six months? One year?
5. How has the MSL role changed since you've been here?
6. Where do you see the MSL function going in the next few years?
7. What is the company culture like?
8. What makes this company unique?
9. What is the biggest challenge for anyone in this specific role (territory) today?
10. What is the biggest challenge facing the MSL team today?
11. What made you choose to work for the company?
12. What are the most important qualities for someone to excel in this role?
13. How would you describe a successful MSL on your team?
14. How will my performance (including success) be measured?
15. How would you describe your management style?
16. What is the next step in the process?
17. What is a realistic timeline for hiring?
18. Have I answered all your questions?
19. Do you have any concerns regarding my candidacy?
20. May I have your business card? (for the purpose of sending a thank-you letter and possibly sending an email with any follow-up questions)

Questions for Other Key Decision Makers

1. How does your department or team interact with the MSL team?
2. On what projects do your department or team and the MSL team collaborate?
3. What do you believe are the ideal qualities that will make someone successful at the company?
4. How would you describe a successful MSL?
5. What is the company culture like?
6. What makes this company unique?
7. What made you choose to work for the company?
8. What do you like best about working for the company?
9. After our discussion today, how do you think I would fit at the company?
10. May I have your business card? (for the purpose of sending a thank-you letter)

Review the suggested questions to ask in Chapter 6 for other possible relevant questions.

At the End of Each Interview

✓ Always thank the individual for their time.
✓ Always express your excitement for the role and the company.

Most Common Reasons MSL Managers Reject Applicants During an In-Person Interview

Over the years, I have seen aspiring MSLs make numerous avoidable mistakes during interviews. These mistakes typically result in an applicant being eliminated from consideration.

Some mistakes frequently made by candidates are obvious (not bringing extra copies of your CV, not knowing all the details on your CV, not turning off your phone, etc.), while other mistakes are not as obvious.

As stated previously, as an aspiring MSL, it's important to be aware of the most common reasons MSL managers do not move an applicant forward in the hiring process. A survey conducted by the MSL Society revealed that "poor communication skills," "poor presentation skills," "being unprepared," and "lack of enthusiasm" were four of the most common reasons MSL managers globally and U.S.-based MSL managers reject an applicant during an in-person interview (Tables 87 and 88). Be sure to avoid these critical mistakes.

Table 87

Survey question: "Typically, during an in-person interview, what are the most common reasons that prevent you from moving an applicant forward in the hiring process (further interviews or an offer)? (Check all that apply)"

Reason for Not Moving Forward – In-person Interview			
Poor communication skills	70%	Inability to address "why this job?"	32%
Poor presentation skills	63%	Using or checking their phone during the interview	32%
Being unprepared	59%	Speaking negatively about current or previous employer, manager, team	32%
Lack of enthusiasm	58%	Poor body language	29%
Being arrogant	53%	Failing to be succinct when answering questions	29%
Unpolished communication	51%	Speaking negatively about the role of sales representatives	27%
Being unprofessional	51%	Does not articulate relevant therapeutic area and/or disease state experience	23%
Being awkward or weird - inability to carry on a "normal" conversation	49%	Not asking relevant questions	22%
Poor cultural fit	47%	Concern regarding frequent job changes	22%
Lack of understanding of the MSL role	44%	Dominating the conversation	21%
Speaking rudely to an administrative assistant or others	41%	Asking inappropriate personal questions	18%
Lack of confidence	38%	Not knowing all the details on their CV/Resume	18%
Provides inaccurate or false details about their academic background, experience, or other details	38%	Inability to address concern regarding lack of or limited MSL experience	18%
Inconsistent answers	38%	Appearing desperate	17%
Lack of connection with applicant	37%	Arriving late or too early	14%
Inability to match background/experiences to the needs of the role	36%	Concern regarding career gaps	12%
Lack of knowledge of the company or our product(s)	35%	Applicant inquiries about salary or benefits	5%
Failing to fully answer questions asked	34%	Other (please specify)	3%
Dressing inappropriately	33%	Not bringing copies of their CV/Resume	2%
Failing to fully answer questions asked	34%	Other (please specify)	3%
Dressing inappropriately	33%	Not bringing copies of their CV/Resume	2%

2018 "MSL Hiring Practices Survey," MSL Society
185 MSL Managers
Global Results

Table 88
Survey question: "Typically, during an in-person interview, what are the most common reasons that prevent you from moving an applicant forward in the hiring process (further interviews or an offer)? (Check all that apply)"

Reason for Not Moving Forward – In-person Interview			
Poor communication skills	68%	Dressing inappropriately	32%
Poor presentation skills	63%	Inconsistent answers	32%
Being unprepared	63%	Poor body language	28%
Poor cultural fit	60%	Not asking relevant questions	27%
Lack of enthusiasm	58%	Provides inaccurate or false details about their academic background, experience, or other details	26%
Unpolished communication	55%	Speaking negatively about current or previous employer, manager, team	24%
Being awkward or weird - inability to carry on a "normal" conversation	49%	Dominating the conversation	23%
Being arrogant	47%	Concern regarding frequent job changes	23%
Being unprofessional	46%	Does not articulate relevant therapeutic area and/or disease state experience	22%
Lack of knowledge of the company or our product(s)	45%	Speaking negatively about the role of sales representatives	20%
Lack of understanding of the MSL role	44%	Appearing desperate	17%
Lack of connection with applicant	42%	Arriving late or too early	16%
Failing to fully answer questions asked	39%	Asking inappropriate personal questions	16%
Lack of confidence	37%	Not knowing all the details on their CV/Resume	16%
Speaking rudely to an administrative assistant or others	35%	Inability to address concern regarding lack of or limited MSL experience	16%
Failing to be succinct when answering questions	35%	Concern regarding career gaps	10%
Using or checking their phone during the interview	34%	Applicant inquiries about salary or benefits	6%
Inability to match background/ experiences to the needs of the role	34%	Other (please specify)	3%
Inability to address "why this job?"	33%	Not bringing copies of their CV/Resume	2%
Using or checking their phone during the interview	34%	Applicant inquiries about salary or benefits	6%
Inability to match background/ experiences to the needs of the role	34%	Other (please specify)	3%
Inability to address "why this job?"	33%	Not bringing copies of their CV/Resume	2%

2018 "MSL Hiring Practices Survey," MSL Society
97 MSL Managers
U.S. Results

The Importance of the Thank-You Email

As stated in Chapter 6, sending a thank-you email is important!

As you may recall, a survey revealed that 71 percent of U.S.-based MSL managers and 51 percent of MSL managers globally indicated receiving a thank-you letter or email from an applicant is "very important" or "somewhat important" after an in-person interview (Refer to Tables 71 and 72 in Chapter 6).

Within twenty-four hours, send a thank-you email to each individual with whom you interviewed with throughout the day. If necessary, review the phone screen section for detailed recommended guidelines for sending a thank-you email. These messages are an effective way to further demonstrate professionalism and an opportunity to reemphasize how your experience matches the specific needs of the role. Each email should be personalized to the specific individual by including key details you discussed during the interview.

The Next Step

If you are successful during the in-person interviews, HR will contact you with an offer letter.

Sometimes, there is a second round of in-person interviews. This is often necessary when a number of key decision makers were not available during the first round, or when the team is deciding between two similarly qualified applicants. If a second round of in-person interviews is required, prepare for it by following all the guidelines and suggestions throughout this chapter. Although the format of the second round of in-person interviews will be similar to the first, it's unlikely you will be asked to deliver another PowerPoint presentation.

8

The Offer and Salary Expectations

If you have made it this far, congratulations! Although reaching this stage—being offered your first MSL role—is exciting, you need to understand a number of details before accepting an offer. Although the order may vary, what follows is what you can generally expect at this stage of the hiring process, along with suggestions on how to successfully accept your first offer.

The Verbal Offer

Typically, someone from HR or a recruiter will first call you to extend a verbal offer. They will share details of the offer, including the full title of the role, the territory (or region), the salary and overall compensation, vacation and holiday time, an overview of the benefits, the company car or car allowance (if being offered), the sign-on bonus (if being offered), and possibly other details. When they are reviewing all the details of the offer, you should take detailed notes to compare them to the written offer. Respond with excitement and thank them for the offer, but *do not accept* the offer over the phone. If you have any questions about what is being offered, write them down and mention you would like an opportunity to review all the details of the offer in writing.

References, Background Check, and Drug Screening

If these were not requested earlier in the interview process, you may be asked to provide two or three references. Regardless of when you provide references, companies will typically contact them only when they are about to make a job offer or when they are considering two final candidates. Although it's a positive indication that you may be about to receive an offer, your references should be able to attest to your abilities that match well with the MSL role and provide a positive character reference. A poor choice of references could result in not being offered the role or an offer being rescinded.

In addition, during the offer stage, you will likely be asked to give consent to the company to perform a criminal background check.

A drug screening may also be required. If it is, the company will typically provide the name of a testing company that performs drug screenings in your local area. You will then need to contact that testing company to schedule an appointment.

Lastly, the company will verify your academic credentials, including verification of degrees and dates of attendance. Some companies may also require a credit check as well.

It's important to be aware that although you may receive and sign the offer letter before a reference check, background check, degree verification, and possibly a drug screening are completed, the accepted offer will be contingent upon successful completion of all company requirements.

Receiving the Offer in Writing

Typically, you will receive the offer in writing within a few days after the verbal offer has been made. Although some companies will send a printed copy of the offer letter via an express courier service (FedEx, UPS, DHL), most companies send the written offer digitally to your email address, utilizing an online document signing service, such as DocuSign. Although there are no specific requirements as to when a response should be received, it's generally expected that applicants will reply within several days.

Components of a Typical Offer Letter

After receiving the written offer, review it carefully. Verify that all the details included in the written offer match what was mentioned during the verbal offer. The written offer will typically include:

- Job title and description or responsibilities
- Name and title of your immediate supervisor
- Start date
- Salary and overall compensation
- Full benefits and eligibility
- Year-end bonus
- Paid time off (holiday, vacation time, etc.)
- Company car or car allowance (if being offered)
- Territory or region
- Relocation expenses (if applicable and being offered)
- Stock options (if applicable)
- Sign-on bonus (if offered)
- Employment status (Typically, MSL roles are considered "exempt" employees, which means they are exempt from certain hourly pay laws and thus not eligible for overtime pay.)
- Other details

If, after reviewing the written offer, you have a clear understanding of all the details and agree to all the terms, accept the offer by signing it.

However, if there are any details you do not understand, or if there are any discrepancies with the notes you took during the verbal offer, contact the individual who made the verbal offer and clarify those discrepancies—prior to signing and accepting the written offer.

In addition, if, after reviewing the written offer, you decide you want to negotiate any detail, it's important to understand that most of the components (including paid time off, benefits, and year-end bonus) are typically nonnegotiable and are set at the corporate level. However, the starting base salary may be negotiable. Before considering negotiating for a higher starting salary, you should research starting MSL salaries to have a realistic expectation. This research will be crucial to successfully negotiating a higher starting salary.

Credible Sources for MSL Salary Information

Regardless if you are considering negotiating or not, it's important to have realistic expectations regarding the starting salary and other compensation for new MSLs. However, researching MSL salaries can be difficult due to the limited availability of accurate and credible information. Although there are a number of online salary research websites, such as salary.com, these websites either do not have any information specific to the MSL role, or the information will be very limited. Typically, these websites also combine salary information for several roles they consider similar to the MSL role, which is not useful in determining an accurate MSL salary.

Due to the limited availability of accurate and credible salary information for the MSL profession (among other reasons), in 2014, the Medical Science Liaison Society conducted the first ever global MSL Salary and Compensation Survey. Since its inception, the purpose of this annual survey has been to gain insights into current global MSL salary and compensation levels across pharmaceutical, biotechnology, medical device, and other healthcare companies. This survey is the largest database of MSL salaries in the world, and the 2022 survey included 2,099 MSL professionals from sixty countries; as a result, it is the most comprehensive, authoritative resource on MSL salary and compensation levels.

The results of the 2022 Salary and Compensation Survey are available in fifteen different versions, including the global report and fourteen individual country reports: Australia, Brazil, Canada, Colombia, France, Germany, India, Italy, Mexico, Portugal, Spain, Turkey, the UK, and the U.S. Regardless of where you are located, the data from this survey will serve as a credible resource and provide a realistic expectation for a starting salary based on a number of variables. Within each report, salary data is segmented by:

- Gender.
- Ethnicity.
- Academic background.
- Years of experience.
- Company type.
- Therapeutic area.
- State of residence (for those based in the U.S.).

In addition to understanding the base salary for MSLs, the reports also provide insights into other types of compensation and benefits as well.

Within each report, data is segmented by:

- Salary negotiation.
- Sign-on bonus.
- Salary increase.
- Bonus received.
- Bonus eligibility.

- Company stock.
- Paid days off.
- Benefits received.
- Benefits desired.
- Salary satisfaction.
- Age range.

MSL leaders also consider the annual MSL Salary and Compensation Survey conducted by the MSL Society to be a valuable and credible resource. In fact, a majority of medical affairs executives both in the U.S. and globally utilize the MSL Society Salary Survey data as part of their benchmark data for determining MSL salaries (Tables 89 and 90).

Table 89
Survey question: "Do you utilize the MSL Society's annual MSL Salary and Compensation Survey as part of your salary benchmark data?"

MSL Salary Survey Use	
Yes	57%
No	35%
I have no knowledge of this	8%

2022 "MSL Salary & Compensation Survey," MSL Society
63 Executive Management/VP of Medical Affairs
U.S. Results

Table 90
Survey question: "Do you utilize the MSL Society's annual MSL Salary and Compensation Survey as part of your salary benchmark data?"

MSL Salary Survey Use	
Yes	55%
No	33%
I have no knowledge of this	12%

2022 "MSL Salary & Compensation Survey," MSL Society
73 Executive Management/VP of Medical Affairs
Global Results

A final potential source of salary information is external recruiters. If you are working with an external recruiter, they will know the salary range for the role for which you applied, and they may be willing to share the salary ranges for MSLs they have placed with various companies.

The Average Starting Salary for an MSL

A realistic starting salary can be difficult to determine. There are a number of factors that are considered in determining what salary you are offered, including your educational background (PharmD, PhD, MD, etc.), geographical location (i.e., country), the type of company (e.g., pharmaceutical, medical device, etc.), and the therapeutic area or disease state the MSL role supports, among other factors.

Although base salaries vary considerably around the world, in the United States, the overall average base salary for MSLs in 2022 was $182,239 per year. However, the average base salary for a new MSL (with less than one year of experience) in the U.S. in 2022 was $160,731 (Table 91).

Table 91
Survey question: "How many years of MSL and/or MSL management experience do you have?"

Experience	Average
Overall	$ 182,239
Less than 1 year	$ 160,731
1 - 2 years	$ 170,010
3 - 4 years	$ 185,115
5 - 6 years	$ 193,903
7 - 8 years	$ 204,972
9 - 10 years	$ 191,783
11 - 15 years	$ 211,702
15+ Years	$ 213,509

2022 "MSL Salary & Compensation Survey," MSL Society
1,032 MSLs/Sr. MSLs (or equivalent title)
U.S. Results

For starting salary data for other countries, refer to the latest versions of the MSL Society annual salary and compensation individual country reports.

Steps to Successfully Negotiate

Prior to attempting to negotiate a higher starting base salary, it's important to have realistic expectations of the outcome, as well as to know the steps to successful negotiation.

Although 75 percent of U.S.-based MSL managers and 72 percent of MSL managers globally revealed that the base salary offered to an applicant is negotiable, surprisingly only 38 percent of new MSLs (those with less than one year of experience) in the U.S. and 36 percent of new MSLs globally negotiated their initial offer (Tables 92–95).

Table 92
Survey question: "Typically, is the base salary offered to an applicant negotiable?"

Base Salary Negotiable	
Yes	75%
No	25%

2018 "MSL Hiring Practices Survey," MSL Society
97 MSL Managers
U.S. Results

Table 93
Survey question: "Typically, is the base salary offered to an applicant negotiable?"

Base Salary Negotiable	
Yes	72%
No	28%

2018 "MSL Hiring Practices Survey," MSL Society
185 MSL Managers
Global Results

Table 94
Survey question: "Did you negotiate the most recent base salary you were offered (even if it was a merit increase for the same company or role)?"

Salary Negotiation	
Yes	38%
No	62%

2022 "MSL Salary & Compensation Survey," MSL Society
167 MSLs/Sr. MSLs (or equivalent title) with less than 1 year of experience
U.S. Results

Table 95
Survey question: "Did you negotiate the most recent base salary you were offered (even if it was a merit increase for the same company or role)?"

Salary Negotiation	
Yes	36%
No	64%

2022 "MSL Salary & Compensation Survey," MSL Society
246 MSLs/Sr. MSLs (or equivalent title) with less than 1 year of experience
Global Results

However, even if you are successful in negotiating a higher base salary, it's important to have realistic expectations. According to the 2022 MSL Salary and Compensation Survey conducted by the MSL Society, when new MSLs (less than one year of experience) in the U.S. did successfully negotiate, they received, on average, a 5 percent increase above the original base salary offered.

In addition to researching and having realistic expectations regarding the starting salary and typical outcomes of negotiations, the impression you make during the negotiation discussions will also contribute to your success in obtaining a higher starting salary. Always remain professional, and base the negotiation on the salary research you have conducted. Avoid using emotional words (e.g., "want," "need," "deserve") or language that may be interpreted as confrontational, which may undermine the negotiation. The use of emotional language can damage your relationship with a future coworker before you even start the job. In extreme cases, the use of confrontational language may result in the job offer being retracted.

The following are essential steps to successfully negotiating a higher starting base salary:

✓ Contact the individual who made the verbal offer (i.e., the HR representative or recruiter) and request some time to speak. Mention you have a few questions regarding the offer and would like clarification on some details.

- ✓ When speaking with them, first express your gratitude for the offer and your excitement to work for the company.
- ✓ Ask if there is any flexibility in the base salary that was offered.
- ✓ If they indicate the original base salary is their best offer, immediately accept the position because your primary goal is to break into your first MSL role.
- ✓ If there is flexibility, indicate the salary offered is lower than what you think is appropriate. Make a compelling, objective case for requesting a higher base salary based on your research into current salary data for new MSLs, as well as the value you will bring to the role.
- ✓ Speak like an MSL by referencing the relevant starting base salary data published in the latest version of the MSL Society's MSL Salary and Compensation Report.

Be prepared for one of the three following possible responses after your request:

1. The company stands firm with the original offer.
2. They increase the offer, but it's still below your expectations.
3. They increase the offer, and it meets your expectations.

Regardless of their response, thank them for their consideration and verbally accept their offer because your primary goal is to break into your first MSL role. When accepting their offer, thank them enthusiastically, and let them know you are looking forward to the opportunity and contributing to the MSL team.

Revised Final Offer and Acceptance

If the company agrees to increase the starting base salary, you will receive a revised written offer reflecting the increased salary. After receiving the offer, carefully review all the details again to ensure they match what you discussed during the negotiation. As with the original written offer, if you have any clarification questions, you should contact the individual with whom you are working—prior to signing the offer. If you need no further clarifications and agree to all the terms, accept the offer by signing it.

Final Thoughts

I hope you have found reading *The Medical Science Liaison Career Guide: How to Break into Your First Role* to be valuable.

A Medical Science Liaison career provides substantial financial rewards, numerous benefits, professional growth, autonomy, and a high level of job satisfaction. As a result, MSL roles are highly sought after, and breaking into the MSL profession is very competitive!

For many applicants, breaking into the MSL profession is a long, rigorous, and highly frustrating endeavor. It's nearly impossible to achieve on your own without the proper preparation and insights into the MSL hiring process.

My goal for this book was to provide you a step-by-step guide on how to break into the dynamic rewarding MSL profession. Throughout this book, I have shared numerous specific techniques and effective strategies for distinguishing yourself from other applicants, including the secrets of how to successfully search for, apply for, interview for, and ultimately break into your first MSL role.

Although it may require multiple applications and interviewing with several companies before you are successful, remaining persistent will be critical to your success.

My final advice is to apply the knowledge you have gained throughout this book and implement the numerous strategies I provided into action.

I wish you the best of luck!

If I can help, feel free to connect with me on LinkedIn at www.linkedin.com/in/samueldyer or via email at samuel.dyer@themsls.org.

P.S. I always enjoy learning about success stories, so if you utilize this book to break into the MSL profession, please let me know.

Acknowledgments

Writing the second edition of this book was exceedingly more difficult and time-consuming than I had initially anticipated, but it was also very rewarding. I would like to thank Jeff Kraemer for his friendship, assistance, and the countless number of hours he dedicated to helping me throughout the process of writing of both editions of this book. Without his involvement, this book would not have been possible. I also want to thank my wife, Heliana, who supported and encouraged me throughout the long journey of writing both editions, despite all the time it took away from other personal endeavors.

I would also like to thank my editors, interior designer, book cover designer, and indexer for their professionalism and attention to detail.

I am very grateful to the hundreds of aspiring MSLs who utilized the first edition of this book to successfully break into their first MSL roles and provided feedback on the content of the book.

Finally, I express my gratitude to the numerous colleagues within the global MSL community who discussed ideas for the book, reviewed sections, contributed insights, and provided support throughout the writing of this edition.

About the Author

DR. SAMUEL DYER is the CEO of the Medical Science Liaison Society and has over 23 years of international MSL experience. During his career, he has managed MSL teams and operations in over sixty countries across the United States, Canada, Europe, Africa, the Middle East, Australia, and New Zealand. He has facilitated the successful launch of pharmaceutical and medical device products for both Fortune 500 pharmaceutical companies and small biotechnology companies.

Dr. Dyer has coached, interviewed, and reviewed the CVs of countless aspiring MSLs. His insights and guidance have resulted in hundreds of aspiring MSLs successfully breaking into their first roles.

While leading the MSL Society, he has conducted MSL training programs for over 50 pharmaceutical, biotechnology, and medical device companies in more than 15 countries. Dr. Dyer has also written extensively on the Medical Science Liaison profession, including numerous published articles, benchmark studies, and reports. He has been the keynote speaker and moderated numerous international conferences on various MSL–related topics, including creating teams, management, MSL training, proper utilization of

MSLs, global trends, and the KPIs and metrics used to measure MSL performance. Dr. Dyer has also served as a resource and consultant on a number of MSL–related projects for several organizations, including McKinsey & Company and Bain & Company.

Dr. Dyer has a PhD in Health Sciences from Touro University and is attending medical school at Washington University (Health & Science) School of Medicine. He has a master's degree in Tropical Biology (where he studied in the Amazon) from Southern Illinois University Edwardsville and has a bachelor's degree in Biology from the University of the State of New York. Dr. Dyer also completed a certificate program for Executive Leadership and Strategy in Pharmaceuticals and Biotechnology at the Harvard Business School.

Appendices

What Is a Large, Medium, or Small Pharmaceutical Company?

As you research the MSL profession and begin to network with those directly involved with the MSL community (e.g., recruiters, MSLs, MSL managers, HR personnel, etc.), you will likely encounter the terms "large," "medium," and "small" pharmaceutical. Although there is no standard definition for what is considered a large, medium, or small pharmaceutical company, it is important to have a general understanding of what these terms mean when researching target companies and applying for MSL roles. Although various criteria (e.g., total market value, number of employees, global revenue, etc.) are used to describe small, medium, or large pharmaceutical companies, the terms are generally based on global annual revenue.

$10+ Billion USD	$1–$10 Billion USD	< $1 Billion USD
Large Pharma	Medium Pharma	Small Pharma

B

Successful
Virtual Interviews

Virtual technology, such as Zoom, Skype, Webex, Microsoft Teams, or other similar platforms may be utilized to conduct interviews at any stage (i.e., phone screen, phone interview, or as a replacement of an in-person interview) throughout the MSL hiring process. As with a phone or in-person interview, your preparation and communication skills during a virtual interview will determine your success. The following are ten essential steps for a successful virtual interview.

1. Test Your Technology

It's important to test your equipment and technology to minimize technical issues. Ensure that you have a strong, stable internet connection, and confirm your webcam, speakers, and microphone are all working properly. If you need to purchase or replace any component, do so well in advance of the scheduled interview. Be prepared to conduct the interview on a laptop or desktop computer, not a mobile phone or tablet.

In addition, be sure the technology being used for the virtual interview is installed and working on your desktop computer or laptop before your meeting. Technology glitches on the day of the interview will convey a negative impression, cause unnecessary stress for you, and will be disruptive to both you and the person with whom you are interviewing.

2. Create a Professional Environment

As with a phone screen and phone interview, it's important to establish a professional environment conducive to a successful virtual interview. The following are several best practices:

- Organize a quiet area free from possible interruptions and without distracting background noises, such as children, pets, music, television, outside noises, etc.
- During a video interview, the space around you will be on camera, so ensure it is clean and organized so that the interviewer focuses their attention on you and is not distracted by what is around you or in the background.
- If possible, position your webcam, so there's a blank wall behind you.
- Ensure you have optimal lighting, and your face is well lit by placing a ring light or a bright lamp in front of you.
- Avoid sitting with a window or bright light behind you.
- If you will be using a laptop (as opposed to a desktop computer), place your laptop on a table or a desk.
- To avoid distractions, turn your mobile phone off or use the silent mode. Do not have it near you.

3. Be Prepared

Many of the strategies for preparing for a virtual interview are the same for the phone screen and the phone interview. Review and follow all the relevant techniques and suggestions from Chapters 6 and 7. The following are a number of specific recommendations for preparing for a successful virtual interview:

Before the Interview

- Determine if you need to create an account or download software on your computer for the technology being used during the virtual interview.
- Be prepared to speak at least fifteen minutes prior to when the interview is scheduled to begin.
- Close your internet browser, your email program, all notifications, and all applications or programs on your computer (laptop or desktop) to avoid distractions.
- Do *not* have a printed copy of your CV in front of you. Having printed material in front of you can be distracting and make you appear unprepared.

During the Interview

- Take notes to capture key points; however, note-taking should not distract you from engaging in the conversation or actively listening. As the interview begins, inform the hiring manager you will be taking notes on important points being discussed.

4. Conduct a Practice Session

Before the interview, ask a friend or family member to conduct a practice session with you using the same software that will be used during the virtual interview. During the practice session, a friend or family member should confirm if they can adequately see and hear you, if there is proper lighting, and how you appear on camera. They can also confirm whether you appear professional, prepared, and enthusiastic, or you appear nervous and awkward. If needed, conduct a few practice sessions, and if possible, record the practice sessions, review them, and make adjustments as necessary.

It's also important that you understand how to use the basic functions of the software, including how to mute and unmute yourself, turn on the video, adjust the volume, and how to maximize the screen size. Although each virtual technology has similar functions, you do not want to discover during the interview that you don't know how to use an important function that will be utilized.

5. Adjust Your Webcam

Properly position yourself on the webcam by sitting far enough back from the camera so that your face and upper body can be seen (as opposed to only your face). Place the webcam at eye level so that you are looking directly into the camera and not down. Your face should be centered and take up about one-third of the screen. Also, ensure your hands can be seen on screen because it can make the interview more engaging. In addition, do not use a virtual background because they typically appear fake and can be a distraction.

6. Project Professional Body Language

As with an in-person interview, projecting professional body language during a virtual interview is critical to making a positive impression and will contribute to your success. However, the technology used for these types of interviews reduces the interviewer's ability to interpret and evaluate your body language. Utilize the following techniques to ensure you clearly and effectively communicate professional body language throughout a virtual interview:

- Greet the interviewer enthusiastically as you introduce yourself, smile, and thank them for taking the time to speak with you.
- Avoid looking at the interviewer on the screen when you answer a question. Instead, ensure when you speak that you are looking directly into the webcam. Doing this will ensure your eyes are aligned with the interviewer.

- Create a connection by consistently making eye contact throughout the interview.
- Always sit up straight in your chair with your head up, shoulders back, and square to the webcam.
- While sitting, your feet should be flat on the floor with your arms unfolded at your sides or resting on a table or desk.
- Throughout the interview, speak clearly, and be aware of the volume of your voice (avoid speaking too loudly or too softly).
- Do not sit in a swivel office chair (to prevent distracting rotation or movement).
- Don't sway or rock when speaking.
- When speaking, occasionally lean forward toward the camera to demonstrate confidence and engagement (avoid leaning too often because it will become distracting).
- While listening, acknowledge the interviewer by nodding to communicate that you are engaged.
- Use hand gestures when appropriate, but keep your movements close to your body and within the frame of the screen (avoid excessive gesturing).
- Do not fidget with your hands.
- Avoid touching your face.
- Smile occasionally, when appropriate.

7. Dress Professionally

Dressing appropriately for a virtual interview is critical in making a positive first impression and will also contribute to your success during the interview. As with the in-person interview, you will be expected to be in business attire for a virtual interview. Review and follow all the relevant suggestions from the "What to Wear" section in Chapter 7.

8. Make a Personal Connection

During a virtual interview, your enthusiasm, body language, and even casual conversations all contribute to your ability to build rapport and a connection with the interviewer. Although it can be more difficult during a virtual interview, it's important to find ways to connect with the interviewer. An effective way to accomplish this is by being prepared to talk about a common interest or personal connection you have with the interviewer. Before the interview, research the hiring manager and everyone else with whom you are scheduled to speak by using the relevant techniques described in the "LinkedIn" section in Chapters 3 and 4.

Conducting this research may reveal information that may be helpful in building rapport and establishing a personal connection with the interviewer. This is an effective way of creating a positive impression and standing out from other applicants.

9. Have a Backup Plan

Although testing your technology and conducting a practice session prior to a virtual interview will help minimize the chances of something going wrong, it's important to be prepared if something unexpected occurs during the interview. The following are a few scenarios for which you should be prepared:

If your audio stops working

At the beginning of the interview, when appropriate, ask the interviewer for their phone number. If your audio stops working during the interview, call them directly. Ask if they want to continue the interview by phone or if they want to reschedule.

If background noise interrupts the interview

If an unexpected background noise (e.g., a siren, construction, etc.) occurs during the interview, apologize for the interruption, and ask for a few moments to address the situation. Then mute your microphone until the noise has stopped before resuming the interview.

If someone enters the room unexpectedly

If someone (or even a pet) enters the room unexpectedly during the interview, apologize to the interviewer and ask for a few moments to address the situation. Immediately mute your microphone and turn off your webcam until the distraction has been resolved.

10. End Enthusiastically and Genuinely

At the end of the interview, express your excitement for the position, and let them know you are looking forward to potentially working on their team. Finally, smile and thank them for taking the time to speak with you. Don't forget to send a personalized thank-you email within twenty-four hours. Review and follow all the relevant suggestions from "The Importance of the Thank-You Email" section in Chapter 6.

C

Understanding Internal and External Recruiters

Internal Recruiter	External Recruiter
An employee of a pharmaceutical, biotechnology, medical device, medical diagnostic, or other healthcare company	An employee of a recruiting company which is separate and independent from a pharmaceutical, biotechnology, medical device, medical diagnostic, or other healthcare company
Supports the internal hiring needs of their company	Supports the hiring needs of multiple companies
Typically has expertise in hiring for a specific department (e.g., medical affairs) or a specific role (e.g., MSL)	Likely recruits for a broad range of roles (e.g., pharmaceutical industry) or may have expertise in recruiting for a specific role (e.g., MSL)
May submit a CV to the hiring manager, even if an applicant does not meet all the requirements listed in the job description	Typically, will only submit a CV to the hiring manager (or whomever appropriate) if an applicant meets all or most of the requirements listed in the job description
May be able to submit applicants without MSL experience to the MSL hiring manager	Often is unable to submit applicants without MSL experience (unless permitted by the MSL hiring manager and/or company)
Has the flexibility to submit an applicant even if the company already has their CV on file	Typically is unable to submit an applicant if the company already has their CV on file

Index

Note: Page numbers in *italics* indicate tables.

A

applicant tracking software (ATS), 108–110

B

background checks, 190
behavioral interview questions, 138, 153–154, *155*, 181
Bing, 91, *91–92*
blockbuster drugs, 27
blogs, pharmaceutical industry, 57
body language, professional, 97, 173–175, 214–215
business attire, 93, 172–173, 215
business cards, 94–95
business information, sources for, 59–60

C

clinical trial information sources, 58
coachability, 178, *179*
Code on Interactions with Health Care Professionals (PhRMA), 22–23
commercial vs. medical education activities, 22–23
communication skills
  CV as a demonstration of, 99
  introductions, 93–94
  nonverbal, 98, 173–175, 214–215
  in-person interviews, 176–178
  phone interviews, 149–151, *151*
  phone screens, 136–137
  presentations, 167–172, *167–168*
company research
  approved and marketed drugs/products, 63–65
  company size definitions, 60, 209
  hiring managers expectations of, 49–51, 61, 64–65
  importance of, *50*, 60–61
  in preparation for in-person interview, 163–164, 175–176
  in preparation for phone interview, 146–148, *149*

Made in the USA
Columbia, SC
23 August 2023

21929013R00134

THE MEDICAL SCIENCE LIAISON CAREER GUIDE

How to Break Into Your First Role

Even for highly qualified candidates, breaking into the Medical Science Liaison profession is a challenging endeavor. It's nearly impossible to achieve on your own without the proper preparation and guidance.

The Medical Science Liaison Career Guide: How to Break Into Your First Role is a step-by-step guide on how to break into the competitive MSL profession. The book provides numerous techniques and effective strategies for distinguishing yourself from other applicants and reveals the secrets of how to successfully search, apply, interview, and ultimately break into your first MSL role. The book also reveals the techniques utilized by 545 MSLs who successfully broke into the profession, as well as the preferences of 185 MSL hiring managers when evaluating applicants.

DR. SAMUEL JACOB DYER shares his years of experience as a hiring manager at some of the world's top pharmaceutical companies and as the CEO of the MSL Society. In three sections, he thoroughly explains the MSL role, provides the elements of a successful MSL job search strategy, and demystifies the entire MSL hiring process. Dr. Dyer has coached, interviewed, and reviewed the CVs of countless aspiring MSLs. His insights and guidance have resulted in hundreds of aspiring MSLs successfully breaking into their first roles.

www.themslbook.com

ISBN 9780989962636

9 780989 962636

90000